"The only one factor that I can positively link to the value of a currency, and I'm not really sure why, is the direct relationship with defense spending,"
Dennis Gartman, Publisher of The Gartman Letter and Fund Manager.

"I think that one will always make a lot of money by betting against the wisdom of central banks,"
Dennis Gartman, Publisher of The Gartman Letter and Fund Manager.

"I cannot stand the hypocrisy that circles the Royal Family, often disguised as criticism. The obsession with one family, as if they either were or ought to be miraculous if only they can behave better, is offensive to me as a rational being."
Sir Samuel Brittan, Assistant Editor, Financial Times of London

"The Monarchy was not much affected by the collapse of Barings, since most of the assets of the Royal family are in shares, trusts or land. They really only keep petty cash in the bank."
Sir Samuel Brittan, Assistant Editor, Financial Times of London

"The recent experience with respect to the pursuit of monetary policy from 1991 to 1993 was a repeat of the errors that the U.S. Federal Reserve made during the years of the 1930s great depression . . . This entire episode was repeated in the 1990s in Europe. Germany convinced most European Union members that inflation was about the only important policy goal to be concerned with."
Paul DeGrauwe, Member of the Belgian Senate

"I see very few attractions to Paris as the main financial centre. If the U.K. participates in a single European currency, there is no question of London remaining the pre-eminent financial centre."
Paul DeGrauwe, Member of the Belgian Senate

"Since 1978, the year that deregulation became official, an estimated 150 new airlines entered into the competitive game, of which 118 declared bankruptcy or merged with other carriers."
Sami Helewa, Jesuit and U.S. Aviation Commentator

"The lessons from the crisis in Mexico are threefold. Firstly, if you are going to have a devaluation, plan it properly. Secondly, have your people on side to talk to the New York bankers about the shift in the domestic economic policy framework, and lastly, don't go on vacation the week after you devalue."
Alan M. Rugman, Thames Water Professor of International Business, Oxford University.

"Americans are notoriously xenophobic. Only 15 percent of American citizens carry a passport. Which means 85 percent don't care much about anything outside of the U.S. There is not a leading community in the U.S. which understands international finance and economics,"
Alan M. Rugman, Thames Water Professor of International Business, Oxford University.

"To be a player internationally, you have to be in Asia. One amazing fact is how few American firms or European firms are competing with the Japanese. In short, Japan is leading world trade and investment which is why the yen is so strong."
Alan M. Rugman, Thames Water Professor of International Business, Oxford University.

"If the Bosnian crisis has shown anything, it is that U.S.-led NATO is the one serious organisation in Europe and any idea of a common EU foreign policy is still very far away,"
Chris Cviic, British Commentator,
Author and Journalist.

"Russia is currently going towards a rather chaotic period of privatisation and transformation. Its evolving into some form of corporatist state . . . with a great deal of flexibility through the element of organised crime."
Chris Cviic, British Commentator
Author and Journalist.

"George Soros has taken up a number of projects that could not have been financed by existing institutions."
Chris Cviic, British Commentator,
Author and Journalist.

"In recent years, we have incorporated several words in our modern language. Terms or euphemisms like globalization, competitiveness, total quality management, derecruitment and downsizing. All these personify in some form or another the "new" political and economic age we live in. The phrase "information superhighway" is a culmination of such thinking."
Jerry J. Khouri, Journalist and Middle East Consultant

". . . while the debate over the Tobin tax, derivatives, foreign exchange markets and other issues rage, traded markets will continue to innovate and grow. If roadblocks are put in their way the markets and the people will move."
Dr. John Pattison, Specialist in Compliance and Regulatory Affairs and Executive, CIBC World Markets

"The Bank of England is a good example of a balanced and cost effective regulatory regime as noted above. Singapore is also a good example. It is regrettable that the Barings episode occurred on their territory . . ."
Dr. John Pattison, Specialist in Compliance and Regulatory Affairs and Executive, CIBC World Markets

"The key structural change variable can be summed up in one word . . . "QUALITY." The Japanese introduced high quality vehicles into North America in the 1980's.
By the end of the 1980's virtually everyone had significantly increased their quality levels."
Dennis DesRosiers, President,
DesRosiers Automotive Consultants

"Overall, we look at our strategy of operation from a U.S. vantage point, as opposed to a Canadian, where our head office is located."
Richard Venn, Chairman and CEO, CIBC World Markets

"When an outsider from Japan receives subsidies in the U.K. to build a new plant, along with an opportunity to hire a young and well-trained workforce, something must be done in Brussels to level the playing field . . ."
Philippe H. Gras, Deputy General Director of Renault

"London is proving that you do not need to have a national industrial base in order to succeed in the financial services business. You can have a weak industrial base and a strong financial market culture. This will become even more pronounced, since the U.K.'s industrial base will become even weaker in the future, and the financial services side even stronger."
Laurent Tréca, Director General, Banexi (BNP)

"... as a general rule, the Deutsche mark and the Japanese yen do well in times of peace, but will be set aside if any real broad conflict were to erupt."
Tihomir Mikulic, Chairman and Director, Kapital Trade

"... the U.S. was always inefficiently organised through massive government defense subsidies to whatever industry they decided to champion."
Tihomir Mikulic, Chairman and Director, Kapital Trade

"There is about $380 billion in real American currency circulating worldwide, and experts say there is at least $10 billion in bogus bills along for the ride. Of that $380 billion U.S. in currency, two-thirds of it circulates overseas- making the detection and confiscation of counterfeits difficult."
B.J. Del Conte, T.V. News Producer and Journalist

"The best regulatory model, and the one that follows simplicity the best is that of the U.K."
Dr. John Pattison, Specialist in Compliance and Regulatory Affairs and Executive, CIBC World Markets

G·7 Books
Published by The G·7 Report Inc.
The G·7 Report Inc., P.O. Box 824, Postal Stn. Q
Toronto, Ontario, M4T-2N7, Canada
E-mail: g7report@passport.ca; tel: 416 699 3530; fax: 416 699 5683

G·7 Books Registered Offices:
Toronto, Ontario, Canada

Printed and Manufactured in Belarus
by: World Wide Printing, 114 Wemborough Road, London, HA7 2EG, UK. Offices in
Minsk, Belarus and Duncanville, Texas, U.S.A.

National Library of Canada Cataloguing in Publication Data

Main entry under title: Political, structural & technological change

Includes index.
ISBN 1-894611-04-7

1. Economic history--1990- 2. World politics, 1989-. 3. Technological innovations.
I. Vukson, William B. Z., 1962-

HC59.15.P653 2001   909.82'9   C2001-900220-3

Visit the G·7 Group's website: www.G7Report.com

Illustration and design by Judy Willemsma, Toronto, Canada

Distributors: Orca Book Services, Stanley House, 3 Fleets Lane, Poole, Dorset, BH15
3AJ, UK. Send all orders via tel: 00 44 (0) 1202 665432; fax: 00 44 (0) 1202 666219
Email: orders@orcabookservices.co.uk

Global Marketing Representatives: Drake International Services Ltd., Market House,
Market Place, Deddington, Oxford, OX15 0SE, UK. tel: 00 44 (0) 1869 338240;
fax: 00 44 (0) 1869 338310; Email: info@drakeint.co.uk

POLITICAL, STRUCTURAL & TECHNOLOGICAL CHANGE

Edited by William B. Z. Vukson

OTHER BOOKS IN THIS SERIES

**From the Collapse of the Cold War
to the Rise of the
Hot High Tech Wars**

Organized Crime & Money Laundering

**Three Investment Stories
under Free Trade:
Portfolio, Direct and
Cross Border M&A**

Emerging Markets & Special Surveys

POLITICAL, STRUCTURAL & TECHNOLOGICAL CHANGE

Edited by William B. Z. Vukson

Edited by William B. Z. Vukson

William B.Z. Vukson was born on June 24, 1962 in Toronto, Canada. He is the founding Publisher and Editor of The G•7 Report Inc., established in 1991, consisting of ten Special Information Publications on global investment risk and the Investors' Newsmagazine available over the retail newstrade in Canada and the United States. Mr. Vukson is also a Merchant Banker specialised in Central Europe and founder of a group of wholesale investment funds called G7Funds.

Mr. Vukson has obtained a B.A. in economics from the University of Toronto, Toronto, Canada, and an M.A. in economics from the Centre for Economic Studies, University of Leuven, Leuven, Belgium.

Edited by William B.Z. Vidson

CREDITS

As the Chairman, Publisher and Editor of The G•7
Report Project, I would like to thank my Editors:
Sami E. Helewa S.J., Jerry J. Khouri, Antonio
Nicaso and Dennis DesRosiers; our specialist com-
mentators: Dr. John C. Pattison, Francesco
Riondino, Lee Lamothe, Tihomir Mikulic, Dr. Alan
Rugman, Andreas Utermann, Paul Nielsen, Dr. Paul
De Grauwe, Alex Constandse Dr. Michele Fratianni,
and our internet site Webmaster: Marshall Heaton.
Finally, I would like to thank Ms. Judy Willemsma,
one of the most efficient Creative Directors that I
have ever had the pleasure to work with.

I would also like to thank Andy J. Wood, Jean-Pierre
Paelinck, Terry Labelle, George Valenta, Raymond
Low, George Vukelich, Marinko Papuga, Al Petrie,
Johan Lambrecht, Chris Cviic, Jayson Myers, Mark
Chandler, James Farmer, Mark A.A. Warner, Frank
Boll, Douglas W. J. Young, Ron Dodds, Joanne
Girouard, Giovanni Giarrusso and all others that
were involved with this project over the past years.

William B.Z. Vukson

Table of Contents

POLITICAL AND STRUCTURAL CHANGE IN THE POST COLD WAR WORLD

HIGH TECH AND INNOVATION ...PAGE 103

PREFACE

This book is related to four other books *(I: "... from the Collapse of the Cold War to the Rise of the Hot High Tech Wars ..."; II: THREE INVESTMENT STORIES UNDER FREE TRADE: Portfolio, Direct and Cross Border M&A; III: Emerging Markets and Special Surveys; IV: Organised Crime and Money Laundering)* and was authored or edited by William B.Z. Vukson throughout June and July of 2000. It is a concise overview of some of the most important recent geo-political and economic developments affecting global commercial strategies, and laying the groundwork for the understanding of the revolutionary decade of globalisation; the "1990s." The focal point for this overview more or less begins in the turbulent 1970s, under a time when OPEC, the Red Brigades and the European Monetary System negotiated by Helmut Schmidt and Valéry Giscard d'Estaing were all evolving. In essence, an attempt is made to account for the revolutionary nature of the 1990s by using the turbulent 1970s as a loose benchmark throughout.

The related series of books referred to above in *italics*, are a collection of articles and interviews that began in January of 1992 and continued until December of 1999, published in *The G•7 Report: Investors' Newsmagazine.* It is an historical and eyewitness account of the period by an eclectic group of writers and contributors. It can be called an "anthology" of the 1990s and a witness to this period of globalisation. Although some articles are five years or older, readers may be surprised to find how relevant the issues are as they have been presented, even today as we begin to progress through the new millennium. Many of the articles and interviews capture the essence of change and help in identifying vital trends and geo-strategic patterns. The policy of *The G•7 Report* and its editors and contributors has always been one of objectivity and neutrality. Many differing viewpoints were encouraged, although readers may get the impression at times, that there was an over-reliance on market solutions to problems raised by the rapid globalisation of markets and technological change.

Although allocation and distribution of income are now determined by a global market more than at any time in recent history, the road ahead may not be so clear. Just as the experiment with unfettered markets collapsed at the end of the nineteenth century, so too may our current globalised market system become transformed in the future. To understand the direction of this future can only begin by examining in great detail the decade of the 1990s.

The G•7 Report Project

FOREWORD

The G•7 Report Project came about unexpectedly. After having spent many
years in academia, trade and merchant banking, I felt that a new communications forum was needed that would bind together an inter-disciplinary
approach to the new developments and challenges faced in this emerging new
decade, the 1990s. As things turned out, the past decade proved to be one of
the most revolutionary periods in the twentieth century, with an unprecedented
combination of global markets and technological invention. All of this called
for a fresh new start in media, research and documentary journalism that
yearned for direction from a unique type of leader; perhaps one that brought to
the table a rare combination of both academic and theoretical grounding, combined with unequalled practical know-how. To be an effective leader or strate-
gist in the 1990s, it was not enough to just be a specialist within a narrow area
of expertise, nor was it sufficient to rely on just many years of "experience"
within a particular sector of the economy.

In this respect, the academic approach to economics and world business was
deprived of what John Kenneth Galbraith once termed as "practical good
sense" evident in great abundance throughout the revolutionary 1990s. Even
within the confines of the "new high tech economy" a great deal is lost in trying to understand the longer term trends that are in play, let alone in predicting
the rise and progress of this new high tech world. Very few Economists in the
early years of this decade predicted what has transpired via the internet, nor
has the profession been too adept at charting the long term trends that have
been emerging in global stock markets, not to mention the currency markets. In
fact, on the latter point, most have dismissed trends in currency markets as
belonging within the sphere of the random walk. Asked where the dollar-yen
parity may be tomorrow or one month from now, the quick reply would have
been "the same as where the relationship has stood at the close of business
today." Asked where it would stand one or two years from today, the answer
would amazingly have been the same. Yes, the new orthodoxy in the 1990s was
the random walk. Under this method of analysing currency markets, there was
no way to predict the short term daily or hourly parities between two currencies, nor was there any strategy to pursue long term risk management of fluctuating currencies.

The name, "The G•7 Report," was derived from an international monetary
economics course that I attended and which was taught by Professor Michele
Fratianni, an expert on exchange rates and interest rates and former Chief
Economist of the European Commission in Brussels and a member of the
Council of Economic Advisors in Ronald Reagan's Administration, not to mention a good friend of mine. Of interest was how both fiscal and monetary policy
was formulated within the industrial grouping of the most powerful economies

in the world, the interaction between them, and the effects a particular direction would have on the emerging market group of countries that border these powerful G•7 nations.

In simple English, if all of the members of the G•7 were expanding fiscal spending or lowering interest rates in concert with one another, the disruption as reflected via fluctuating exchange rates would be kept to a minimum. This would be of particular benefit to all parties transacting international business, since strategy and planning within organisations find it most difficult to hedge the effects of gyrating exchange rates. On many occasions, the serious financial press is full of reports of disappointing earnings results due to financial hazards that have impacted subsidiaries in various parts of the world.

The initial attempts to co-ordinate official demand-creation activities within the G•7 have been motivated to a large extent on purely trade grounds. Liberalised capital mobility and the burgeoning "herd-mentality" lead by some well known hedge-funds is a phenomenon that arose in the early 1990s, through George Soros' glorious victory in ejecting the pound sterling out of the European Exchange Rate Mechanism, which was the prelude to the present day single currency- the Euro. However, in the mid 1980s, the hey-day of G•7 policy co-ordination exercises, it was trade concerns which were at the forefront of the policy debates.

After Francois Mitterrand's Socialist Party took power in 1981, politicians in France broke with their G•7 counter-parts in order to pursue a massive re-inflation which ultimately proved very short-lived. To break from the pack in such a manner, the French franc nose-dived in global currency markets as inflation skyrocketed upwards. The Mitterrand government quickly learned that individualistic approaches to policy were dead ends, and that the short-lived expansion quickly made the exchange rate attractive to foreign buyers, but that the ensuing price increases, or inflation, choked off the gains that buyers would have had from the lower franc. In short, the "Mitterrand experiment" exacted great inefficiencies on fellow member G•7 nations and had limited real impacts on the domestic French economy. Mitterrand quickly retreated from this approach and agreed to become a team player thereafter.

Not only were such policy directions between the world's most powerful economies vital in understanding how business cycles interact between these countries, but a collective decision to increase spending or to lower interest rates exacted a real impact on the global economy, and the emerging market countries in particular. During the transformation of Russia and the former communist countries of central and eastern Europe, many have argued in favour of a concerted G•7 expansion in spending and their creation of a more global demand that would in turn assist in the transformation to a market system. This criticism remains valid as trade and investment flows from the G•7 to *the newly emerging market economies and vice-versa, has been disappointing, hence prolonging the transformation process and creating more hardship than what would have been otherwise necessary.*

The G•7 Report project was not just about economics and business, but was a new vehicle that introduced a number of journalists and commentators unfamiliar to the readers of the daily news in major North American cities. We retained some leading contributors over the years, such as Harvard Professor Benjamin Friedman, Belgian Senator and leading international trade Economist Paul De Grauwe and compliance and regulatory expert Dr. John Pattison, but also introduced numerous writers that would normally not have had the opportunity in the commercialised or market-driven media to express their views and communicate with our readers. We became known as a media that was made available to some leading European based journalists such as Italian based organised crime expert, Antonio Nicaso, and to his counterpart in Canada, Mr. Lee Lamothe, the former head of the crime section of the Toronto Sun daily newspaper.

The G•7 Report project attained a small "niche" circulation in major North American cities such as New York, Boston, Miami, San Francisco, Los Angeles, Toronto and Montreal, but was never able to develop a following in places such as Vancouver or Atlanta. Moreover, throughout 1995 and 1996 we were also available over the retail newstrade in the City of London at selective newsagents. Furthermore, The G•7 Report project was not something that was developed by marketers residing in New York, Toronto or Los Angeles. In fact, I would be the first to stick my neck out and say that this was among very few recent launches which went the other way around. I did not "measure" or "test" the market with this concept before launching the product. In essence, The G•7 Report made and shaped its own following and market over the years. It was a leader which was embraced by a very loyal grouping of reader, that felt that we had important things to say about global trends and the rising "new economy."

The G•7 Report project was particularly foreign to advertisers, especially among the agencies in Toronto. We counted very limited success in soliciting advertising support, and agency calls and presentations tended to border on the absurd. In short, The G•7 Report was simply not a concept that was welcomed within this realm. Most of the major corporate supporters were much appreciated, yet very rare. Among this select group, we are very grateful to Ford Motor Company, the Montreal Stock Exchange, NatWest Markets and Kapital Trade as our core group of advertisers. The problem that any "niche" publisher must go through is retaining a core group of supporters over the long term. If this can not be maintained, then the publication either dies or gets transformed over the years. We greatly relied on the latter technique to ensure our survival. However, it was interesting to note that we did not deviate much from our core group of readers, regardless of the format of The G•7 Report. Since 1992, we went from an academic-looking journal to an expensive full-glossy magazine, to a newsprint version and ending with the current newsletter look. We found that the constant throughout this entire process of transformation in design were our core readers over the years, and for this we thank them for their ongoing and unbending support.

William B.Z. Vukson

POLITICAL AND STRUCTURAL CHANGE IN THE POST COLD WAR WORLD

POLITICAL AND STRUCTURAL CHANGE IN THE POST COLD WAR WORLD

These are probably some of the most prolific articles that The G•7 Report project has ever published. When the Berlin Wall collapsed, people around the world felt a conflicting sense of fear, as well as optimistic anticipation as to what it all meant. Many were left speechless, such as French President Francois Mitterrand, who could see major changes in attitudes taking place almost immediately within Europe. The U.S. Administration of George Bush was relegated to the role of spectator, able only to utter vague statements in support of what seemed to be developing in Europe.

Once the support blanket of the Cold War was gone, events that seemed unreal at first took centre stage. The move by Italian Magistrates, led by Antonio Di Pietro in Milan, to indict some of the highest ranking business and political leaders on mafia association charges and corruption was a clear signal that the new rules of the game were now taking shape. No country in the G•7 was more a bridge between the west and the communist east, than was the Cold War politics of Italy. The U.S. had no greater a man supporting their interests in the southern Mediterranean, than that of the former seven time Prime Minister of Italy, Giulio Andreotti. When Andreotti was put on trial by Italian Magistrates, it signalled the end of the Cold War.

Furthermore, as former Socialist Prime Minister, Bettino Craxi fled to exile in Tunis, he left clear evidence that embezzlement of party funds had occurred in Swiss banks, which would ultimately expose the power politics played out with some of the highest profile businessmen in Milan and Turin. None other than Carlo De Benedetti of Olivetti and holding company Cir, was called to account for his dealings with the former Socialist Premier, as Silvio Berlusconi's Fininvest empire was also placed under investigation for a countless trail of kickbacks with political leaders throughout the Cold War years.

Italy, in this respect, has always been a crossroads to the world of Communism, which was hanging right over her eastern border town of Trieste. Needless to say, a proper inquiry into the causes of the Collapse of the Cold War must always go through Milan, Turin and Rome for one to fully understand the conflicting special interest groups that were unique to the Cold War system. The G•7 Report early on, presented an exclusive "scoop" interview with the powerful Giulio Andreotti that was conducted in Rome by leading organised crime specialist, Antonio Nicaso. In my judgment, Andreotti's downfall and the trial on Mafia Association that ensued was the most important event that signalled an end to the old system of power politics. In that respect, we thank Giulio Andreotti for allowing us direct access during one the most difficult times in his career and life.

"French Watergate" was inspired by the growing power of Italian Magistrates, as Prime Minister Edouard Balladur, was being investigated for granting French police the authority to bug or eavesdrop on conversations of political adversaries in an almost Nixonian manner.

"A Fighting Dollar" was an interesting interview with leading financial newsletter writer and fund manager, Dennis Gartman, on how military spending exerts a leading effect on the strength and direction of the U.S. dollar. Frustrated with a lack of evidence from financial variables like interest rates, Gartman's theory was very timely in light of the massive structural changes occurring in the 1990s.

W.b.z.V.

Exclusive Interview
Giulio Andreotti's Moment of Truth

Interview with: **Giulio Andreotti**
Directed by: **Antonio Nicaso**

He speaks of dark sinister plots and stubborn allegations that he lived his public life in the private pockets of the Sicilian Mafia. "I may be a bad Christian, but I could never have had dealings with people who kill", says Senator Giulio Andreotti, seven times prime minister of Italy and life-long politician. As stacks of criminal indictments-totalling more than 16,000 pages- pile up around him, the 76 year-old statesman tries to remain above the fray. Accused of using his prestige and power as one of the great influential political leaders of his country, Andreotti denies links to the Cosa Nostra. The Public Prosecution of Palermo has compiled the massive dossier tying Andreotti to the most horrible of crimes: the Sindona case, the slaying of Roberto Calvi, the Mafia assassinations of his friend, Salvo Lima, and of anti-Mafia General Carlo Alberto Dalla Chiesa. Another allegation is that Andreotti holds information about the kidnapping and murder of Aldo Moro, the statesman of the Christian Democratic Party, who was targeted by the Red Brigade. The Palermo file contains hundreds of testimonies, records of ongoing investigations, photographs, wire tappings and eavesdropping transcripts, and analysis of a range of organized crime allegations from earlier trials. They soak Andreotti's inquiry like custard in a cake. Andreotti has tried to remain above the allegations. But in an interview given for a forthcoming book, he spoke of intrigues and plots, of sinister motivations by the United States: "Why do they do this in America, I don't know. There are shadowy surroundings which I have firmly fought. In the area of drug trafficking you find Sicilian/Americans; of course they have strong powers."

All of your collaborators associated with people directly linked to the Mafia or to those close to it. Did they ever warn you against the dangers of that type of environment?

It may seem strange, but that's the way it is. If it weren't for the informants then my non-involvement would be crystal clear. Informants that speak now, after years of testimony and questioning. Here we have a prompter. Foreign secret service, splinters of services, Sicilian and American Mafia, I cannot distinguish among them, I can only assume.

In the indictments there is a statement of a former American prosecutor, Richard Martin: "In 1985 Buscetta said to me: in order for you to understand the difficulties I have in talking about the links between Mafia and politics, I will say one name: Giulio Andreotti."

Mr. Martin has stated that he submitted a report to his superiors. So why then was I cuddled so much by the [George] Bush administration? Why did [George] Schultz call me to the University of California, where he was going to teach, when he left the State Department? Indeed, it was 1985.

Well then...?

It was the year of the Achille Lauro [Italian registered ship hijacked by terrorists in 1985]: Relations between ourselves and the American secret service were very tense. There was the after effect of the Grenada invasion. The Americans did not forewarn us and I gave the go ahead to vote against the invasion in the United Nations.

You have often said that there is a concealed organization overseas. Listen to this one: on December the first, during a public conference, an historian on strategic national studies, Brian R. Sullivan, said: "It seems certain that between 1946 and 1947, De Gasperi, Italian prime minister at that time, nominated his trustworthy collaborator, Andreotti, so that he could be the link to the Mafia."

Nonsense. I may even be a bad Christian, but I could never have had dealings with people that kill. These are people who confess, as if twenty homicides were nothing. The truth is that the Public Prosecution of Palermo, after turning me inside out like a sock, has come up with nothing. I hope that after two years of investigation and sufferings, all of this will amount to nothing. It is no one's defeat. I am sorry for the mortification that has been inflicted upon me. On the moral front, after so many red carpets, a little humiliation has done me good. On the political front, of course, this story has caused great damage to me. I could still have been useful to my country.

Events Leading to the Indictment

• Public prosecutor of Palermo Giancarlo Caselli requests initial authorisation from the Italian Senate to open the case against Giulio Andreotti

• request to stand trial made by Palermo Magistrates in June, 1993

• Magistrate Agostino Gristina will decide if enough evidence exists to prosecute for allegations of Mafia association in a preliminary hearing in Palermo

• hearing has been already twice postponed since October, 1994

• Public prosecutor Caselli may appeal if judge Gristina rejects case on lack of evidence

• Evidence offered by 17 former Mafia figures are under the Witness Protection Program

Exclusive Interview

Interview with: **Antonio Nicaso**
Directed by: **William B.Z. Vukson**

What kind of a politician was Andreotti? What was his record like in Italy over the years?

He was in power for the longest time in Italian history, spanning some 50 years. He started after the second world war as a Secretary of State, with the then prime minister de Gasperi. Afterwards, he was minister of Defense and External Affairs. Presently, he is a life Senator and up until 1992, was in power as prime minister. I think that he is an interesting man, who has a high level of intelligence and many connections in the world. Also, for many years, he was the main political reference for the US in Europe.

What is so special about Andreotti?

He has the ability to go through a fire and not be burned. He has always been able to derive a consensus within his coalitions on vital issues and maintain power in crises. Overall, he is a very astute man and an Italian politician with a high profile on an international scale.

During his time as prime minister, what policy initiatives can be readily identifiable with him?

He looked after the interests of the NATO alliance. He was one of the first to believe in a Europe within NATO. He always believed in European unification and within Italy, he believed in a liberal market system. He always referred to the US as his reference point on this latter point.

Is the US always his first country of reference?

He was one of the most important European politicians that always upheld US interests within Europe.

What other European leaders did Andreotti most identify with?

One of his most fiercest enemies was Margaret Thatcher, because of their differing vision over Europe. Alternatively, former German Chancellor, Helmut Kohl, was the closest European politician to Andreotti.

Is there a special reason for Andreotti to become identified with the Mafia?

The rule of the Christian Democratic Party in Sicily was strong and one of the main members within this party was Andreotti's friend, Salvo Lima. He was killed in an ambush in 1992, and was a member of the European Parliament at that time. On many occasions, there were rumours about him on his links to organised crime, which Andreotti always defended as having no basis in evidence.

The important aspect to the whole situation is that the power of the Lima faction in Sicily always supported Andreotti within the Christian Democratic Party. Moreover, his faction in Rome together with the Lima faction within the Christian Democratic Party, became the joint power brokers and ruled over all of Italy for the longest of time.

Also, one of the biggest problems for Andreotti was Lima. Now, the charge against Andreotti, was that Lima, according to the Magistrates, was the political reference of the Sicilian Mafia. And through Lima and Andreotti, the Mafia was able to exert influence on trials that were taking place against its own members in Rome. This is the prime accusation against Andreotti.

On that basis, many informers testifying against Andreotti, claim that they have seen Andreotti together with the boss of the Mafia in Sicily. Personally, I am not judging anyone, but I decided to write a book on Andreotti as a witness to recent Italian political events. In our interview, I asked him everything about this case just as a prosecutor would. Andreotti answered all of my questions.

Obviously, I got his version, and some of his arguments were convincing and others not. Some of the accusations against him are inconsistent. For example, some informers' accusations are factually incorrect, according to the records. I wanted to reveal to the people the defense of Andreotti, in his own words, without passing judgment of my own. I am not a judge.
What is his main defense?

That the informers against him are encouraged by unknown Americans. According to him, some special lobby decided to eliminate him from the international scene, based on the fact that there no longer exists a threat from the former Soviet Union. In other words, since no communist threat exists, Andreotti is no longer important to the interests of the US.
So Andreotti was used against the spread of communist ideology?

Some Magistrates believed that the Christian Democratic Party used its Sicilian Mafia links to contain the spread of communism within Italy, and believed that the Mafia played a large role in the Yalta summit, after the allied victory in the Second World War. The Christian Democratic Party used the Sicilian Mafia to halt the spread of communism. Andreotti denied this in our interview.

Accusations against former Prime Minister Bettino Craxi sent him into exile in Tunisia, yet Andreotti stayed in Italy. Does his act of remaining in Italy not reflect some degree of innocence?

No, they are two different cases. With Craxi, enough evidence exists of his embezzlement of party and state money to Swiss bank accounts. Meaning, they have direct evidence in his case against him. Andreotti's case is very different because there is testimony from former members of the Mafia. It is their word against his. The Magistrate in this case must determine which side is telling the truth. There exists no direct evidence against Andreotti in this case, as in the Craxi case.

Why have Magistrates gone after politicians suspected of wrong-doing now?

It is very strange that the action is now, yet everyone knew of certain wrong doings in politics perhaps ten years ago or more. The timing of the actions of Magistrates is a mystery, since they knew of the wrong doing and corruption in Italian politics some ten or twenty years ago.

What is the view of the current politicians that are in power, such as Lamberto Dini, Silvio Berlusconi and Gianfranco Fini about the Andreotti case?

They are all very silent!

Giulio Andreotti was interviewed by editor Antonio Nicaso in his Rome office from November 1994 to January 1995. The entire interview was published in Italian in the book: "Io e la Mafia"- La Verita di Giulio Andreotti.

FRENCH WATERGATE
Balladur's Past Begins to Resurface at a Critical Point

Antonio Nicaso

It is not the first time this has happened in the history of the French Fifth Republic. Is the curse of the Elysée claiming yet another victim? In the collective imagination of the French people, the Elysée is the palace of the father-figure of the country. The man who lives there is between two fires: when the people love him, it is almost carnal; when they hate, their loathing is often visceral. They are not capable of normal, moderate feelings. There is no indifference or disinterest. Witness two previous victims of the Curse. In 1974, former President Jacques Chaban-Delmas fell after his inaccurate income tax return was published in a tabloid newspaper. Next up, and down, was Valéry Giscard d'Estaing who in 1981 accepted diamonds from Central African cannibal Emperor Bokassa. Is this the same curse that haunted Prime Minister Edouard Balladur, until a few weeks ago the front-runner as successor to Francois Mitterrand? The latest polls show Balladur's standing has plummeted in the wake of allegations of a dirty little police probe targeting a relative of an anti-corruption judge.

Anyone going before the French people has to be pristine, even virginal, in his pursuit of the country's highest office. The voters clearly respect a candidate's morality over his political platform. It is a reflection of a society that believes in the primacy of ethics over politics. The massive wave of love that can carry a candidate to victory can easily turn into the flood that drowns him.

This mentality goes back to the days of General Charles de Gaulle. It was he, in 1962, who wanted the head of the French Republic to be elected by universal suffrage. He understood, long before the others, how important it was for the French people to participate in the election. It was not only a question of introducing an element of democracy directed in the Constitution of the Fifth Republic, but to promote the dialogue with the citizens, the complicity of people-oriented power. This is why the Bonapartism of de Gaulle has taken the shape of a "Republican Monarchy." Although he was a national hero, his political policies were harshly opposed. But his ethics have never been questioned. France was at his feet because there was a guarantee that ethical values would be interpreted, whether good or bad. The true greatness of de Gaulle was in his supreme disinterest for all material aspects of political life. The French loved him more for his ascetic characteristics than for his political institutions.

Once de Gaulle was off stage, France did not change. It has remained as demanding as before. The French have sustained presidencies that were ethically questionable. However, when they could vindicate themselves at the polls, they did with a vengeance. The cases of Chaban-Delmas and of Giscard d'Estaing are symbolic. They both had political character to stay at the Elysée. However, they did not win public opinion because they blatantly betrayed the Gaullist legacy. Perhaps their faults were not very harmful, but it was an indication of opportunism that did not coincide with the presidential ethics.

Now the wrath of the French people could fall on Edouard Balladur. No one in France would assign to prime minister a moral stature equivalent to General de Gaulle. But until recently, everyone recognized his style. The fact that he has allowed himself to be mixed up with the eavesdropping scandal has greatly clouded his image. Is it possible to crown someone who consents to a dirty police operation? With the French voters going through their hate-cycle-- and the numbers clearly show Balladur sinking like a stone-- the one who might gain the most at the polls is rightist Jacques Chirac, the mayor of Paris.

A FIGHTING DOLLAR
As Defense Spending Falls So Does the Dollar!

Interview with: ***Dennis Gartman***
                      Publisher of The Gartman Letter &
                      Private Fund Manager

Directed by: ***Tihomir Mikulic and William B.Z. Vukson***

What is the main factor affecting the value of a currency?
Among several factors, the political one is the first. No one is going to invest capital in a country where the investor perceives the political risk in doing so very large. Having said that, I find very little correlation over time between the fundamental current account balances and a currency. I have seen current account balances become positive and have their respective currencies decline, and I have also seen current account balances become negative, and still have their respective currency values decline. I have not seen any correlations either with the balance of trade numbers. Nor do I see any real correlation among nominal and real interest rates. People tell you that interest rates help to guide currencies, but I do not believe it since history does not give me any evidence as to that effect. The only one factor that I can positively link to the value of a currency, and I'm not really sure why, is the direct relationship with defense

spending. Countries that have stronger defense spending in terms of its proportion to GDP, tend to have stronger currencies. I can speculate, however, that this relationship has a connection with political strength.

Defense spending can also have a very powerful effect on the overall levels of economic activity in an economy, as it had with the US?

Basically that is true. Most of the defense spending in the US is internally created, which has a ripple effect throughout the entire economy. In California, which is the largest defense contractor in the union, the ripple effect from Boeing and other such larger aircraft manufacturers, has a very strong effect in the entire region, stretching from Washington state in the north and down to Nevada and Arizona in the southwest.

Would you say that this relationship holds stronger in the US as opposed to other G7 countries?

I would say that this relationship is stronger in the US and has been strong historically in both of the UK and Canada, but has not been as strong in Germany or in Japan. However, it may become a very important factor in Japan over the next few years, as the Japanese are expected to increase their defense expenditures and have this component take a much larger share of their overall GDP. There is a large movement in Japan at this very moment to change its constitution to spend more on defense, since the Japanese are very sensitive to developments across the Sea of Japan towards China and Russia, concluding that political risk is on the rise in these areas. Therefore, the correlation is not as strong in Europe as it is in the United States.

Why do you think that defense spending is going to go up in the United States over the next five years and take the dollar with it?

For one, I think that the US understands that it is the dominant world power, and that the responsibility for keeping peace around the world does fall on its shoulders primarily, and it realises that no one else is really prepared to take over such a role in a serious way. Moreover, it has run down its defense capability to inordinately low numbers over the past four years. Despite what most liberals will tell you in the US, defense spending as a percentage of GDP is at its lowest level recently and has stopped going downwards. Probably this will begin to reverse due to our ever expanding role in foreign affairs.

In what way would a Kemp-Dole Republican administration be different than the continuation of the current Clinton-Gore Administration when it comes to the value of the US dollar?

It's interesting since Bill Clinton's policy so far has been very dollar supportive. If you would have listened to most economists during the 1992 presidential election campaign, and well into the term of Bill Clinton, they would have argued that the current Administration would have been devaluationist. Instead, his Administration has continually stated that a stronger dollar is to the benefit of most Americans. Moreover, Treasury Secretary Rubin's comments have been very pro-dollar.

How would a Kemp-Dole Administration affect the value of the dollar?

I think that Jack Kemp has been a clear supporter of a strong dollar in the past. However, Bob Dole's comments on the value of the dollar have been very few and very far between. I have tried to research what Mr. Dole has said about the value of the dollar during his term as Senator, but have not been very successful. However, it can be said that with the exception of Ronald Reagan, most Republican presidents in the past have tended to be dollar devaluationists, which is contrary to what most people would have expected.

How would a supply-side tax cut possibly affect the value of the dollar?

Supply-side economics under Ronald Reagan has contributed to a very strong dollar. Also, in New Zealand, the policy that is pursued with emphasis on tax cutting, has given very good support to their dollar. In the case of the UK, when Margaret Thatcher's Conservative government adopted very strong supply-side tendencies, the pound sterling strengthened. I think that the overall tendency is to have a stronger currency under a supply-side, tax-cutting regime.

There have been reports over the past summer of the successful co-ordination policies that the world's main central banks have pursued in maintaining relatively stable exchange rates among the dollar, yen and the Deutsche mark. Are you a believer in the power of central banks when it comes to engineering foreign exchange markets?

I think that one will always make a lot of money by betting against the wisdom of central banks. I don't buy the fact that central banks have somehow entered a brave new and "credible" world. I think that the wisest central bank at this moment is the one that is in New Zealand, and they openly state that they have no idea where their dollar is going to go. The US Federal Reserve has absolutely no idea about what to do with its reserves, whereas the Bank of Japan continues to squander away its reserves at will. I just see no wisdom emanating from these institutions. What has contributed more to stability in the currency markets has been governments bringing their budgets into line, instead of any arguments that may give central banks this credit.

You are optimistic on the Canadian dollar based on its fundamentals?

Absolutely, I think that budget deficits are getting into line and the referendum problem with Québec has been pushed away by at least another four years, and industry in Canada has made itself much more competitive.

Is the Dow Jones overvalued, or is it an unexplainable "demographic" effect which is behind the current record valuations in stocks?

I have a very difficult time with the US stock markets, because whatever fundamental financial ratio that one looks at, makes the value of stocks preposterously overvalued. At this moment, I have a very difficult time in trying to be bullish on equities. I can understand the inflows of cash going into the market from the on-going demographic shifts now occurring in the United States, as the population ages. However, I see greater value elsewhere, and will continue to put my money in these alternative areas.

Can we just dismiss these recent record highs on the Dow as being a cause of the current demographic trends, or can there be another explanation for it?

I think that demographics have a great deal to do with the current highs. We are getting to a period of time historically, when this huge flow of baby boomers is beginning an incredible shift of capital towards savings, and as they get older they will become more and more conservative and put more pressure on their governments to pursue conservative policies. Consistent with this trend, I think that the United States has done a great job in making its industry respond to this shift of capital, by making its corporations more leaner and efficient. However, despite these trends, the Dow Jones still seems to me to be quite high at this point in time.

Some media reports have started to add pressure on the over-valued Dow Jones average, likening it to the frenzied period which preceded the big crash on Wall Street in 1929. Do you share similar views on the current state of the Dow?

I think that people are smarter now than in 1929, and there is a better general awareness in the public on basic issues of economics than there was back then. In that respect, the public's overall propensity to panic is much reduced than what it used to be. Are stocks high? Yes. Are they at 1929 levels? Yes. Can stock prices go down in the United States? Yes. Do I think that ten years from now stock prices will be lower than they are right now? Yes. Do I think that they will go down swiftly, perhaps crashing at once? No. I think that it will be a very slow and long bear market, but I really do not know when this trend will start.

You do believe that a bear market is on its way?

Absolutely, just like night follows day, and morning follows night. When will it come? It may come when the US Federal Reserve has moved the yield curve into an inverted position, where short term rates are higher than long term rates. Until then, the risk of a bear market happening on substance is relatively limited.

How far of a dip in the Dow Jones do you foresee?

Historically, when a bear market begins, it usually takes away anywhere from 30 to 60 percent of the value of the stocks from where they were prior to when the bear market officially set in. This is the best that I can share with you about such a scenario at this point in time.

What can you tell us about the likely direction of the price of gold ?

I have absolutely no desire to be either long or short on gold. I have absolutely no interest in holding bullion at all. I just don't think that the gold market is worth paying any attention to at this point in time. For example, just the country of Belgium could supply the world's gold needs over the next six years just to bring it in line with the gold holdings with the other central banks in Europe. Just the supply held with the Belgian central bank is enough to keep gold prices from rallying.

INTERNATIONAL ORGANIZATIONS AT THE MILLENNIUM
New Reforms that Address Congressional Hostility

Michele Fratianni and John Pattison

As the millennium approaches, few of those involved in international financial and economic affairs pause to consider that today's system of international organizations was created in the 1940s out of the economic and political concerns of the depression and the Second World War. The system was created by an international political process that was unique to the 1940s, for a different membership of major nations, to solve fundamentally different economic, political and security issues. Far fewer realize that there is a basic mathematics of cooperation that dominates practical issues of economic, financial and political relations.

On the other hand, far more people worry about the random topical applications of these two points. Examples are concerns over the Asian crisis and the role and prescriptions of the International Monetary Fund, the increasing isolationism of the United States and its related impact on individual international organizations and processes; the importance of large third world economies and the imminent role of a new Europe with a single money in search of its global financial role. Critics of US foreign policy comment on the lack of focus after the cold war or the growing role of US interest groups, such as the Cuban vote, as reasons why the United States often takes a narrow position on matters of broad international significance.

While much of this analysis may have useful insights to offer, we see these as symptoms of a much greater set of issues. In the work which we have been doing since the 1970s we have stressed the underlying economic forces which have the same effect on international economic cooperation, as supply and demand have on determining prices. The further the world economy gets from the analytical origins of the current system, the greater are the underlying forces making international cooperation less likely and less effective.

The Economics of Cooperation

In the late 1940s, the United States' share of the benefits of cooperation was greater than 60 percent. This was 60 percent of the output of a fairly small industrialized world. This provided a convincing and politically acceptable case for extensive international cooperation in general as well as a case for the United States investing in the costs of cooperation. There were many specific examples ranging from the Marshall Plan to the design of the core international organizations that exist today. However by the late 1990s, the United States share has been reduced to a much lower level. This is now perhaps 30 percent of the size of cooperative benefits from the original postwar club, which was essentially Western Europe, Canada, the United States and Japan. If the growth of the Asian tigers is considered as well as the other large countries such as Brazil and China, the equation would suggest that the United States, and in fact all other countries, would have little incentive to initiate international coopera- tion. This is because none of them are large enough to appropriate enough of the benefits, particularly relative to costs to play a meaningful leadership role. This is very different from the postwar situation and a factor that is usually ignored.

Another way to look at this situation is to look at it as an oligopoly where the individual countries' shares of cooperation are similar to companies' market shares. In a world dominated by an oligopoly of the United States and a small number of other dominant countries - the situation that existed in 1945 - there were strong incentives not only for cooperation but to initiate cooperative - car- tel like- actions. In an atomistic world where there are a large number of coun- tries, equivalent in market terms to agricultural production, for example, no individual producer has an incentive to lead.

The Crisis in International Cooperation

The conclusion is that the world has been facing a major crisis in international cooperation and that the institutional design and membership of the major organizations needs to be reconsidered. The importance of the mathematics underlying cooperation is that those who focus on particular failures of cooperation are not only going to misunderstand and misconstrue the problem, but will not provide a suitable framework for systematic reform.

For example, those that rail at the US Congress for its attitude towards international organizations are correct, but they miss the point that the underlying analytical issue is that the US can neither get the benefits it once got from international institutions and international cooperation, nor can it profitably initiate many types of cooperation from the, admittedly narrow, viewpoint of the economic calculus.

Part II
One Solution: An Inter-bloc International Organization

Our proposal is that the world needs an inter-bloc international organization. Our analysis illustrates that those organizations composed of many countries offer less probability of success in international cooperation. This can be seen in big bodies such as the United Nations. Moreover some smaller organizations such as the OECD have expanded membership with apparently little thought as to what their market was or what brought value to members. The reason they did so was to expand their budgets and to offer more individual products to more nations. While this was successful, it did not have a palpable effect on the important goal they were originally designed to achieve - incremental international cooperation.

The major point is that we have two economic worlds converging and conflicting at the same time. One is the world of traditional international organizations with membership, voting rules and other paraphernalia often designed for earlier years and different problems. The other world is that of regional trading arrangements (RTA) such as the European Union and the North American Free Trade Agreement (NAFTA), not to mention the Forum for Asia-Pacific Economic Cooperation (APEC) and many others.

These worlds are truly conflicting. For example as GATT floundered, RTAs flourished. The 1994 Annual Report of the International Monetary Fund listed 46 regional trade arrangements started on or after 1986. It appears that 12 more may have been created in 1995. So as cooperation becomes mathematically less probable among large groupings, countries have resorted to regional blocs as a type of solution. Such regional blocs have re-established local oligopolies and hence have re-created the favourable economics of cooperation, but in a local setting. These worlds also converge, but in doing so they create inefficiencies. Take for example the cooperation among the major industrialized countries. Of the 29 member countries of the OECD, 15 are currently members of the European Union and three are countries that have applied for membership in the European Union. Hence EU members dominate the OECD. Why meet in Bruxelles and then reconvene in Paris?

The world, particularly the economic world, needs to create an inter-bloc organization. There is a genuine risk of RTAs replacing the multilateral cooperative processes since many RTAs have success or the promise of success on their side as more effective local oligopolies. Hence it is important to place regional issues into an institutional structure for the benefit of all countries. The large organizations cannot do so because of their increasingly atomistic membership that erodes the favourable oligopolistic environment necessary for success. The European Union, NAFTA and Asia account for perhaps 90 percent of world GDP and a similar but perhaps somewhat smaller share of merchandise trade. Hence little progress can be made on many issues without clear inter-bloc negotiations.

One benefit from such an inter-bloc international organization is that greater success and lower economic and negotiating costs can be incurred when agreements are based on sequential decisions. By segregating the players into groups where all participate but at different stages, better agreements can be created. For example, the members of the European Union would first make their decisions subject to a number of clearly defined conditions, facts, covenants and so forth. Thereafter, Europe would negotiate with NAFTA and Asia in this forum. Where it becomes clear that negotiations are coming to grief over fundamental regional differences, they would at least be clearer in such a setting and would allow greater transparency and hopes of resolution. Today such inter-regional issues may be properly identified or they may be immersed in the larger politics of international cooperation.

The OECD - Our Choice for an Inter-Bloc Organization

The OECD seems best placed to play the inter-bloc role. The European Union, NAFTA and Japan represent 93 percent of OECD membership. Since the OECD is currently becoming more unfocused and running into greater difficulties in creating the types of cooperation among the industrialized countries that it was set up to provide, such a move would be welcome.

The counter argument is that it is easier to create a new governmental body rather than reform an old one. We reject this on several grounds. First, the OECD has changed its membership and function successfully in the past when confronted by fundamental changes in its marketplace - the market for cooperation. It can do so again. Secondly, it would be inefficient and unwelcome to allow the growth of more international organizations without dealing with the lack of success and focus of the existing ones such as the OECD.

Conclusion

If this proposal is accepted there are other steps that would follow. For example, cooperation within Asia would likely need to be enhanced, although that is happening already. Another example is that Canada, the United States and

Mexico would likely need to find new institutional ways of dealing with their markets and policies. A more pressing issue is who would represent areas such as South America? Many of these steps might be considered by some observers to have merit on their own. However, the reality is that an inter-bloc organization is necessary to optimize benefits and to create an environment in which cooperation can occur. Otherwise the self-interest of individual countries and the mathematics of cooperation will lead to an increasingly atomistic, fractious and uncooperative world.

EUROPE IN THE 1990S

Europe was where the real action was happening throughout the 1990s. Not only was the single market coming to completion, but the collapse of the Cold War raised the immediate prospects of enlarging the union. Not to mention the fact that by 1999, a single currency eventually to be called the "Euro" was to be launched, changing the way in which business is done across the entire continent.

In the interview with Peter Ludlow very early in the decade, I could sense the discomfort throughout this period of change that leading academic and political figures were facing on a daily basis. After the currency crises hit the Exchange Rate Mechanism in 1992, questions over "will there be monetary union," were the daily buzz around Brussels. Ludlow may have overreacted to a number of questions during the interview, but in all fairness and in retrospect, a lot was at stake for his organisation during the road to monetary union in the 1990s.

The French perspective was communicated by one of the most competent diplomats in the foreign service, Yves Doutriaux, who also had first hand input in the entire Maastricht Treaty drafting process in 1990, and who also wrote a book about it in: "Le Traité Sur L'Union Européenne." It is interesting to note that he rejects enlargement of the Union to Turkey in the interview.

The "Official View" is an article prepared by the Governor of the Bank of France, Jean-Claude Trichet, who will takeover as the President of the European Central Bank in Frankfurt in 2002. This article goes into more technical details as to how the transition to monetary union will develop.

The interview with Sir Samuel Brittan of the Financial Times of London is entitled: "For Monarchy and Single European Currency," and is an interesting account of the road towards the single currency from the angle of a British pro-Euro supporter. For someone that is a part of the British establishment, Sir Samuel's views on the role of the monarchy and Europe work to enhance the stability of the U.K.

The interview with Belgian Senator Paul DeGrauwe reveals a dissenting view over the approach taken by Europe towards the single currency. The fact that deflationary economic policies were unnecessarily imposed via targets on deficits and debt levels, pushed the overall economic climate in the first half of the decade perilously close to that seen during the Great Depression years of the 1930s in the United States.

W.b.z.V.

INTERVIEW: POST COLD-WAR EUROPE

Interview with: **Peter Ludlow,**
                         Director,
                         Centre for European Policy Studies (C.E.P.S.)
                         Brussels, Belgium

Directed by: **William B.Z. Vukson**

How do you view the potential eastward expansion of the European Community (EC) and how may that impact on existing EC affairs in general?

One must make a distinction initially as to whether enlargement will or whether it ought to occur. I believe that it ought to happen as rapidly as possible, however, I don't believe it will as there has been a very definite cooling among those EC governments who have been keen on enlargement towards eastern and central Europe, with particular emphasis on the British. One must ask why? There are several reasons which I take very seriously, but do not accept. The first is that we have a lot of problems of our own in relation to the Maastricht Treaty and we need to get our own house in order before we can consider enlargement to countries which are problematical in a way that the

EFTA (European Free Trade Association) countries are not.

The second reason is also very serious and if the Visegrad countries (Poland, Hungary and Czechoslovakia), as they are called would become part of the EC, the present deal which was struck in context to the association agreements in 1991 would require revision. This agreement basically envisages the free-trade of goods by the end of the century on an asymmetrical reciprocity, but which specifically exclude steel, textiles and agriculture from the main provisions. Steel and textiles will be brought in, but there will be many doubts as to when or how agriculture will. If you went into full membership negotiations in effect, free-market access would have to be applied and extended, and there would be no question at all that it would be painful for certain countries and sectors within the EC.

The third reason is that enlargement would cost quite a lot of money in two ways. First of all, these are relatively poor countries and they would need financial transfers of the magnitude that Portugal, Spain, Ireland and Greece benefit from. And you could be quite sure that the Spanish and the Greeks would not allow the others to take their money away. It would have to be *en plus*, or additional contributions. Here we are talking about large sums and the biggest sum of money would be needed for an extension of the Common Agricultural Policy (CAP). As Poland, Romania and Hungary are major or potentially major agricultural producers.

The final reason is that any enlargement would alter the institutional balance in terms of the voting structures. So these are the reasons as to why the existing members have cooled-off. And even the British who were previously in favour of setting a date are now saying never. If you look at a recent speech that the British Prime Minister had made as the President of the EC in London on September 7, 1992, you could see that a definite picture of postponement was conveyed. Now, I believe that this is highly regrettable.

Would the process of enlargement aggravate present divisions in the EC. For example, I have in mind the situation where Germany unilaterally against the wishes of the EC recognized the independence of the former Yugoslavian Republics of Croatia and Slovenia? And in general, what are your views concerning the increasing German pre-occupation with eastern affairs at the expense of the Community as is?

This is simply North American romanticism. First of all, the Germans are not preoccupied or infatuated by the east. The east is a great problem and not a romantic dream to cost, and in no way is it a benefit. And the Germans at the moment have only an interest in spreading the burden because of their own problems in eastern Germany. This is just romantic dribble to imagine that.

As far as Croatia and Slovenia are concerned, two things come to mind. First, it wasn't as simple as that, the movement away from Serbia was much more general and was not due simply to German pressure. It was due to the behaviour of the Serbs. The recognition of Croatia did not occur because the Germans wanted it so, even though it was clear that the Germans were pushing for it right from the beginning and much before June and July, 1992.

However, what one can say is remarkable is that it took a long time for the EC to centre on the German position. In the end, the Germans lost their patience and delivered an ultimatum in effect. But the EC was already moving toward that direction, so it was a far more complicated process.

Finally, on Slovenia and Croatia, they will not be admitted to the EC for a very long time. That is not because they are undesirable; but you cannot really envisage a situation where Yugoslavia is picked-off bit-by-bit in favour of enlargement in the EC. I think that the preoccupation in terms of enlargement at this moment is centred on the so-called Visegrad countries of Poland, Hungary and Czechoslovakia.

I do not know when this will happen, and I don't think that the Germans will try to do anything unilateral on this. The Germans are undoubtedly more in favour of enlargement partly to spread the burden. It is not clear to me that the Germans will be able to, or possibly want to push their EC partners toward it. And as I said, I would personally like to go much faster and develop a convergence program leading to full membership for all those that at this stage would qualify by, say, 1998 or 1999. But that is a minority position of which I doubt that many Germans in positions of responsibility take such a similar view.

Would it be a fair statement to make that what is critical to a successful economic and monetary union as well as enlargement in the EC is a good relationship between France and Germany?

The relationship between France and Germany has always been fundamental to the EC. However, I do not think that one should exaggerate it. I think that you would want to see, for example, where leadership over the next few months is going to come from on various matters. I do think that it will come from Bonn and Madrid, rather than Paris. Paris at the moment has serious domestic political problems that will persist until the Parliamentary elections. But the Spanish are emerging now as very strong advocates of pursuing a more aggressive attitude towards Maastricht and the Danes. The relationship between Bonn and Madrid is becoming more important, although I would be the last to say that the Franco-German relationship is no longer important. But at the same time, don't exaggerate it.

The ERM (Exchange Rate Mechanism) approach to EMU (economic and monetary union) has suffered a great setback over the last few months. In retrospect, do you have any reservations to this approach to eventual economic and

*monetary union in 1999? Or could another alternative to the ERM be more
effective?*

I think the ERM approach is the right one and I think it has been very successful. It came under immense pressure for a combination of reasons, of which
some were temporary and others more fundamental or structural. The temporary being the political disturbances post-Maastricht, while the structural being
the fact that over time several currencies had become seriously over-valued.

Secondly, the post single-market speculative capital movements in Europe are
very hard to resist. Now, what has happened in terms of values removes that
fundamental problem, as now there is no longer a need for speculators to be
resisted in principle at any rate, since the causes of their speculation have largely been eliminated- with the Pound and the Lira being devalued.

What was disturbing about the present crisis, and largely the fault of the British
is that a perfectly normal and desirable re-alignment was transformed into a
crisis with the entire European Monetary System. And here the contrast
between the British and the Spanish position is very striking. Where the British
asked for the suspension of the system as a whole, the Spanish line was that we
must devalue and remain within the system.

Now the Italians in the general crisis were also shaken out of the system, but I
am confident that they will re-enter and in 1993 there will be a re-constituted
ERM on a stronger basis because the currency parities will be more realistic.
The only question will be if the British would be a party to it? What will
decide that will be how Mr. Major holds out in the Maastricht crisis. Secondly,
you talk about 1999, but I would like to advance 1997 for a very simple reason,
and that is that under the Maastricht Treaty, you need a majority of States. But
we won't be 12 members in 1997, we will be 16 or 17 with the newcomers. All
of them, with the possible exception of Switzerland, either have or will likely
qualify. So, I don't think it will be 1999, rather 1997, and I believe that the
ERM approach is fundamentally alright.

*The German Bundesbank has maintained throughout that the ERM was an
adjustable system, why was this not better communicated to the other members
in light of the most recent currency crisis?*

I think that you have to see this historically as prior to 1987, not only were
realignments allowed but they took place periodically, and some were quite
significant indeed. The reason that the system was "hardened" in the last five
years is quite complex. Partly it was political, as there was a commitment to
monetary union and, therefore, and wrongly so, any movement within the parities was construed as a diminishing commitment to it.

There were other rather technical reasons, which are not unimportant in this respect. The greater risks of speculative movements coming about due to greater capital mobility was harder to manage once you gave the impression that realignment was possible. I think it was wrong to give the impression that re-alignment was totally impossible, but I can understand why this built up.

If you announce that you can change our exchange rates, you undermine the whole credibility of the system. I would not be too critical of the ERM, but I would be critical when it became quite clear that the rates prior to September, 1992 could not be maintained. Then what should have happened was an agreed re-alignment, as had occurred in early 1982, but the British messed this one up totally by requesting a complete dismantling of the European Monetary System (EMS).

Is it not true that under a regime of near perfect capital mobility, as was the situation, a fixed system of exchange rates especially in recessionary times with member states having different business cycles could not be sustained?

Well, it's difficult, but not impossible!

What interests me is the lack of communication throughout the EC, when the Bundesbank has openly announced that the ERM should be considered as an adjustable-peg system throughout. How do you view this?

Yes that is true, but it may have had something to do with political and technical reasons.

Now that several of the currencies have fallen out of the ERM, does this mean that a two-speed road to EMU is inevitable?

First of all, there has always been a multi-speed road to EMU. Even within the ERM itself. The fact that fluctuation bands ranged from 2.25 to 6 percent indicated a two-speed approach. Secondly, Maastricht itself allows the stronger to go ahead. It would be absurd to do it in a way that told the others to go ahead while some wait. The goal is to develop a game plan to go forward and which allows the strongest to lead and to arrive at a harder system, but which does not decouple that system from the others, because its crucial to the credibility of domestic economic management of all of these countries that they are linked with the hard currency zone. And to urge them to get their house in order is to misunderstand the whole mechanics of the EMS process.

For countries such as Italy and Spain, the credibility of these governments depends on the link to the European framework. So, you must preserve the European framework, but, as we have always had within that single framework, the strong may go faster than the weak, but the weak must obtain help from the strong in order to progress. This is all reflected in the convergence plan within the Maastricht Treaty. I am in favour of a hardening of the inner group, but it cannot at the same time exclude the soft group that has dropped off over the last few months.

Several European commentators have always held the view that the European Economic Community is synonymous with Germany. How would you respond to that?

It is total nonsense. Germany, because of its central position in Europe, and its size is a major economic player. But, France is an enormously important economy, whose present economic fundamentals are stronger than Germany's. In terms of inflation, government expenditure and general economic management; and if you want to have a competition to see which European country is the best governed, I would find it very hard personally to choose between Germany and France.

Helmut Schmidt, the former Chancellor of west Germany, argued back in 1978 when he created the EMS that Germany needs Europe as much as Europe needs Germany. Germany is a very important member of the EC, but it does not run the Community, partly because its government is too inefficient to do so. The fact is that Germany does not operate very well. In the European Council, the German government is really not, in fact, a well organized player. So, I don't think that this model of German dominance or hegemony bears with reality. That is not to say, however, that German fiscal mismanagement does not pose a problem to us all. Certainly, bad management in a major economy causes troubles, but it does not mean that they run the show.

The Maastricht Treaty with its convergence criteria displays a deflationary bias. If we look at it historically, can we not interpret Maastricht as a document which was greatly influenced by the anti-inflationary philosophy of the Bundesbank?

Again, you must look at it from the inside and not just in purely mechanistic terms. The German economy was the best managed in the 1960s and 1970s. Many commentators concluded, and in my mind quite rightly, that one of the secrets of German success stands from its institutional arrangements and the priority it gave to the battle against inflation rather than growth. So, here you have the strongest economy in the EC; and what happened that was largely true with the EMS was the internalization of the German model if you like. But it wasn't the imposition of the German model, it was the internalization. People were not told by Frankfurt as to how they should behave, rather they chose to behave in this way. With the result now that you have the Germans themselves with a loss in credibility by their mismanagement of the unification process. And as I said, in many ways the French economy is now running better than the German. In essence, it is much more German than the German economy.

With the recent round of speculative pressure, where Sterling has fallen out of the ERM. An outside observer interpreting the events could conclude when comparing the reaction of the Bundesbank to the attack on the Franc and Sterling, that it's support on behalf of Sterling was not as even-handed. How do you view this situation?

It reflects realities. The Bundesbank made no secret of the view, which many others shared, that Sterling came in at an unrealistically high rate. It was perceived by many that Sterling had been overvalued from the moment that it entered and had become progressively overvalued over the course of the last two years. Whereas, nobody could argue that the French franc was overvalued.

The decision of the Bundesbank to defend the franc and not Sterling was purely a reflection of those fundamental economic realities. And those fundamental realities in terms of the exchange rate reflect the fundamental economy. Whether they like it or not, the British have one of the weaker economies in Europe, and an economy which has been significantly eroded by government over the last ten years or so. Poor Mr. Major right now is picking up Mrs. Thatcher's bills. So, I don't see this as being a preference for the French over the British. Rather, its a preference for the strong against the weak, and is a reaction that is perfectly natural. You simply don't defend the indefensible!

Looking at the EC budget at 1.2 percent of total community GDP (Gross Domestic Product) seems to me as too small to run such an enterprise as the EC. Members should be willing to allocate more of their GDP to the Community, what is your view on this matter?

That again fails to grasp the major attitudinal shifts in the 1980s about the role of government, and public expenditure in particular. In the mid-1970s people to some extent, while looking at countries such as Canada and the United States with quite different histories, argued as you just did: that you can't have a federation without at least 7.5 or ten percent of GDP being spent at a federal level. Now, the sort of vision of government that lay behind this argument was that government had a major re-distributive role and that it needed a critical mass of funds to engage in this type of demand management.

As you are well aware throughout the west, the assessment of government's role in the economy everywhere underwent significant change, as a more monetarist view of the role of economic policy prevailed everywhere. And this inevitably affected the European Community as well. Now, that general ideological shift is fundamental as there was a new critical attitude; and a new very good critical attitude towards public expenditure in general terms.

But the second fact of which the importance is very easily missed or underestimated is that the European Union is based on a union of mature member states. Where most of the expenditure functions are already well established and administered through the member states. So the priorities in the integration process became those of ensuring that a level playing field existed.

In terms of the poorer countries, the combination of the budget and the subsidized loans through the European Investment Bank (EIB) are very significant. For example, five to ten percent of Portuguese GDP is accounted for through transfers from the rest of the EC. Transfers either through the structural funds from the budget or through the form of subsidized loans which could not be raised in the capital markets.

So, there has been a reduction in the general evaluation of the role of the budget as an instrument of policy integration, and secondly, you have a far more targeted budget than what you had previously. The combination of these two, I think, means that we have a much more efficient approach to public expenditure at the Federal level than what you would have in Canada or what one might say exists in the United States.

But parallels are misleading because in Europe we are uniting on the basis of mature member states. The EC is building on mature national administrations which will remain the main spenders and taxers. And the role of the EC is to co-ordinate and ensure that competition is not distorted, and to ensure that a stable macro-economic environment exists. Now, this is a very different concept of the role of government. It's a very important government role, but also a very different concept.

What are your views on the present impasse in the GATT rounds?

I think it would be highly desirable if we can finally reach an agreement, not only for the EC and North America, but more importantly for the third world. I would argue against any suggestion that the fault is principally that of the EC, but should be more evenly distributed in relation to agriculture. In relation to negotiating tactics, I think that the isolation of agriculture as being the absolute central feature of the whole Uruguay Round, of which everything else stood or fell was itself a major political error at the beginning. It is a design fault of the Round.

Overall, I don't think that anybody is innocent, nor do I think that anybody in particular is to blame. What will happen? I suspect that we will all muddle through to an agreement, but my own view which may be outdated by the time you get to press, is that there will be no progress until we have a change in administrations in the United States or a clarification of the political situation in France, which will not come about until the general elections in March of 1993.

Then you are frustrated by the French position?

No, you are jumping into North American genders. I can understand the French position, as they have already agreed to the heavy adjustment costs in the existing Common Agricultural Policy (CAP) reforms. And I can understand the

French political problems, just as I can understand those of the United States. It is cheap to blame anyone because politics is what it is.

The United States agricultural lobby is also extremely powerful and reactionary if you want to put it in terms of free trade. It is not a case of attributing blame, but of trying to see what is possible and politics is the art of the possible, or the art of compromise. And to turn on France like this is to commit the cardinal error and to make sure the thing would not work. I can assure you that the EC will certainly not gang up against France. So to propose such a scenario is simply cheap North Atlantic; Anglo-Saxon journalism. A fundamental error that the British and others have made is to underestimate the reality of EC solidarity. The EC will not split on the GATT; the GATT might break on the EC.

Who would the EC rather deal with, Clinton or Bush?

I don't know.....

Conducted by William B.Z. Vukson on October 30, 1992 in Brussels, Belgium.

EUROPEAN ECONOMIC & MONETARY UNION: A FRENCH PERSPECTIVE

Interview with: **Yves Doutriaux,**
                      French Ambassador to the U.N.

Directed by: **William B.Z. Vukson**

French Monetary Policy

What is the significance of the newly-established independent Bank of France?

It means that the Bank of France is now more in line with the German Bundesbank and the U.S. Federal Reserve in terms of its structure. It is also in line with the prerequisites of EMU and is similar in structure to what the future European Central Bank ought to look like.

The newly-independent Bank of France has virtually fixed the value of the franc back to its pre-crisis level vis-a-vis the Deutsche mark, by imposing very high interest rates. Is this policy not harmful to the French real industrial sector?

Fortunately, we have had a decrease in our official rates since last year's crises, although according to the business sector, it is not enough. We hope that we will have other opportunities to reduce official rates further, provided that the Bundesbank also co-ordinates such reductions with the Bank of France. There is currently much debate around the strong franc (francfort). Certainly, the past historical experience in France concerning currency devaluation, has never resolved the unemployment problems for which they were usually intended for. Devaluations have also been the main cause of our high recorded inflation rates in the past. At this stage, the policy intentions of the French government are one of maintaining monetary stability, and allowing interest rates to decrease, if possible. The current policy of the newly independent Bank of France is very much in line with this goal.

Yes, but how can you communicate this stance to a French industrialist given the deflationary climate that exists presently?

A high level of co-operation between the monetary institutions of France and Germany, can ensure further decreases in interest rates that satisfy industrial interests.

Is it fair to say that such a level of co-operation has not been attained yet?

It has been very slow in coming. However, in the near future, there is hope for further rate decreases.

With the whole issue of currency values and the francfort policy in particular, is the French position very different from the Anglo-Saxon view as to the role in which a currency value might play in the broader economic goals of a country?

I would not look at it in terms of two different points of view, or two different theories: French vs. Anglo-Saxon. France, due to historical experiences of devaluation, feels that a higher level of stability is required in currency markets. In addition, this is the kind of stability that we would like to see established inside the vast European market. Moreover, this is consistent with the views of many economists and our main trading partners.

With the European Monetary Institute (EMI) (the forerunner to the future European Central Bank) just recently established in Frankfurt at the start of 1994, do you foresee any possible friction occurring between the EMI and the Bank of France or Bundesbank as the EMI slowly begins to assert control over monetary policy on a European scale?

Initially, the EMI will not control monetary policies of European countries, its mandate is to pave the way toward monetary union. Eventually, I envision the functioning of the European structure in a similar respect to that of the U.S. Federal Reserve. In that respect, each existing European central bank would assume the role of a regional bank- as in the case of the New York Federal Reserve bank; the Federal Reserve Bank of St. Louis and so on.

Maastricht Treaty Negotiation: An Insider's Perspective

What was the prime motivation behind the convergence criteria initially?

The convergence criteria was set up to prepare for EMU, at a time when the priority of all governments was to fight inflation. However, due to the present global economic downturn, most European countries are unable to fulfill the original criteria. This, however, still remains to be evaluated at the end of the decade, when all of the original criteria for convergence will be re-interpreted.

To reiterate, the convergence criteria is susceptible to change by re-interpretation of the economic environment at the end of this decade?

By 1999, the European Council will make a political decision. It is then up to them to take any political interpretation required, taking into account the original construction of the Maastricht Treaty and the actual original figures of the convergence criteria.

How were the convergence figures arrived at initially?

Each delegation in the Maastricht negotiations proposed their own convergence criteria. But, I would say that the conservative position presented by the Bundesbank was heavily taken into consideration.

The criteria as it stands was primarily established by the Bundesbank?

No, it was the result of an overall negotiation under the then prevailing economic circumstances, which were very different from those today.

Were the eventual criteria that were agreed upon close to France's negotiating position?

Yes, we were in line with these criteria, but I should add that other countries would have preferred a more lenient set of targets for convergence.

European Enlargement

With the recent additions to the EU of Sweden, Finland and Austria (pending successful referendums later in 1994) and possibly also Poland, Hungary and the Czech Republic, what is the ultimate eastern frontier for a united Europe?

According to the Treaty of Rome, Europe is a geographic notion which ceases to exist at the Ural mountains in central Russia, where the Asian continent begins. Having said that, it is easy to understand that it would be difficult to split one country into parts, since Russia is more than a European country. Furthermore, other notions deal with such concepts as respect of human rights, democracy and free markets. All potential EU members must adapt to these fundamental concepts before they are formally granted membership status in the EU.

What is the southern frontier? Will Europe ever include such countries as Turkey or the north African states?

No, but that does not mean that we cannot expand trade relations, or negotiate economic and political association agreements with these countries. Keep in mind that Turkey has already applied for membership a while ago, but its application is a difficult issue given the political and economic state in which it is presently in.

Conducted on March 31, 1994 in Toronto, Canada.

OFFICIAL VIEW
Europe From a Central Bankers Perspective

Jean-Claude Trichet

The member states of the European Community are now engaged in an historical process of monetary integration. The treaty on the European Union has been ratified democratically by 15 countries. It sets out a clear objective: the installation of a monetary union, a single monetary policy and a single currency. The objective of monetary union serves the fundamental needs and interests of the European economy: Indeed, the future of Europe hinges, in part, on the success of the single market; and, for several reasons which I will address later, there is no such thing as a real single market without an appropriate monetary organisation and, ultimately, a monetary union. Further, the objective of monetary union is being pursued in a progressive, realistic and pragmatic way, within the framework of a process which involves the active participation of central banks.

The European Single Market

The removal of all tariff and non-tariff barriers to trade and investment is no doubt a major achievement of the single market project. It has already brought about, and it should continue to bring about substantial benefits to European economies and, therefore, to European workers, investors and consumers. With its 15 countries, its 370 million inhabitants and its 6 trillion ECU GDP, the European Union now constitutes a unified market which is larger than the US and quite similar in size to the North American Free Trade Area (Nafta). The so-called "size effect" of the single market greatly benefits European competitiveness, activity and, therefore, job creation capacities.

The free movement of capital, which is an integral part of the single market project and which has been enshrined in the Maastricht Treaty, allows for a more efficient allocation of savings and investments. It ensures that firms, as well as other economic agents can raise capital on the best possible terms. Last, but not least, the single market is one of the powerful vehicles we have at our disposal for facilitating the integration of the Eastern part of our continent into the European mainstream, and for promoting the development of our Southern Mediterranean neighbours. The prosperity of all these countries is, indeed, a condition for our own prosperity.

These advantages are crucial, especially if we are to ensure that Europe's legitimate interests are effectively taken into account in a world of economic superpowers. However, we should not take it for granted that these advantages will necessarily materialize, in any full and lasting way, without further progress towards monetary union.

Capital Market Development

An appropriate level of exchange rate stability has always been considered indispensable in the framework of Europe's endeavours to create a more unified economic area. In 1957, when the Treaty of Rome was signed, the disciplines entailed by the international monetary system set up at Bretton Woods were still effective, and capital markets were much less integrated than today. However, the Treaty already stipulated, in article 107, that each member state should consider its exchange rate policy as a matter of common interest.

Currently, the various national economies of the European Union are more integrated than ever. For instance, Germany, the UK, Italy and France, to say nothing of smaller and even more integrated economies, each carry out between 50 and 64 percent of their external trade with their EU partners. It is also worth noting that this integration is no longer just the consequence of the traditional process towards the international division of labour; it is, increasingly, the result of the ongoing constitution of a unified economic area, where similar products are being exchanged, and where direct investment creates complex and durable links between national economies. In such a specific context, wide fluctuations in exchange rates are tantamount to invisible barriers which may call into question the existence of the level playing field and, over the medium term, the concept of the single market itself.

Such drawbacks clearly point out the limits of a single market without an appropriate monetary organisation. But, one must also consider the various advantages that will be derived from the irrevocable fixing of exchange parities and from the single currency itself, with a view to strengthening the basis of European prosperity. The single currency will put an end to transaction and hedging costs for intra-European operations; it will deepen European financial markets and increase their efficiency and their liquidity; it will facilitate the transparency of information which is needed to achieve optimal competition; it will decrease Europe's vulnerability to external shocks; it will help promote Europe's interests in the framework of necessarily strengthened global monetary cooperation.

Fixed Exchange Rates

Erratic exchange rate fluctuations are not only economically inconsistent with the concept of the single market, or even with the concept of the common market, but they are contrary to the present provisions of the Treaty of Rome. An appropriate monetary organisation is, therefore, necessary to deal with the currency relationships within the area covered by the common market, now the single market. That is why the European monetary system was created, with economic convergence as the basic concept underpinning its stability.

On top of the European monetary system and its exchange rate mechanism, which correspond to the so-called first and second stages in the terms of the Maastricht Treaty, monetary union itself appears simultaneously as a crowning of the convergence process, on the one hand, and as a new and powerful means of fostering the best possible functioning of the single market, on the other hand. In order to be fully justified and to deliver its economic benefits, monetary union must have appropriate entry conditions and be based upon appropriate behaviours. The conditions are the famous Maastricht criteria which, in the eyes of all central bankers, cannot be altered or loosened. There are two reasons for this:

• First, it would not be in the interests of the best performing countries and economies to envisage any debasement of their single currency due to the influence of economies which do not meet the Maastricht criteria. Such a situation would undermine currency credibility and, therefore, imply higher market interest rates and lower growth in the single market.

• It would equally be a mistake for an economy which was not fully prepared, in particular as regards the required low level of inflation, to join the single currency area. Indeed, such an economy would rapidly lose competitiveness within the area of the single currency and, would therefore, progressively suffer from poor growth and weak job creation.

It is thus in the common interest of all parties concerned to fully respect the entry criteria of the Maastricht Treaty.

Single Currency Dynamics

Once the single currency area is created, appropriate behaviour by all economies concerned is also necessary, for exactly the same reasons which led to the formulation of the entry criteria themselves. Inappropriate behaviour by a particular economy in terms of public finances, inflation and competitive position would not only be a burden on the other economies belonging to the single currency area. It would also directly hamper this economy which would, by definition, be prevented from regaining its lost competitiveness through currency realignments.

I know that this last remark explains why a number of persons in the UK are sending strong "caveats" vis-à-vis the single currency and stage three of the Maastricht treaty. As far as I am concerned, I will class myself among those who are confident that the single currency area will function smoothly, once it is created, with high levels of growth and job creation, provided vigilance is properly exercised:

• vigilance as regards to the meeting of the entry criteria
• vigilance on the part of the European System of Central Banks in accordance with the Maastricht Treaty
• vigilance on the part of the Council of Ministers in implementing the provisions of the Maastricht treaty when they call for action to be taken in case of excessive public deficits
• and, above all, vigilance on the part of each particular economy concerned, in order to preserve its competitiveness in the interests of its own growth and job creation potential

For the sake of the sustainable growth of the single currency area and of the creation of stable jobs, I trust such vigilance will be fully exercised, in a spirit of responsibility, not only because it is called for by the text of the treaty, but because at stake is the obvious common interest of all parties concerned.

The objective of monetary union is being pursued in a gradual and pragmatic way, with the close involvement of central banks. The entry into monetary union depends, first, on meeting five convergence criteria, namely: inflation, long term interest rates, currency stability, public deficits, and outstanding public debt. These criteria correspond to generally accepted principles of good and sensible economic management and sustainable growth.

I would like to dwell on the first of the five convergence criteria: price stability. The monetary union, the future European system of central banks (ESCB), and the future European central bank (ECB) will aim at price stability. Indeed, most European countries have achieved, over the last decades, a high degree of price stability. European monetary union must, and will, foster, not jeopardize, this hard-won achievement. To this effect, the Treaty stipulates that price stability will be the ESCBs primary objective. Economic theory and empirical observation suggest that achieving this objective will be a major contribution to sound growth and to the creation of stable jobs, which is the legitimate, ultimate aim of any economic policy. I would say that, as things stand today, the process of monetary integration is facilitated by the very wide consensus which exists, in Europe, on this objective of price stability.

Indeed, international comparisons tend to prove that, over the medium term, independent central banks tend to deliver greater price stability. My feeling is that, in the increasingly volatile and unpredictable financial environment, central banks must be clearly perceived as poles of stability. The Treaty on the European Union provides that the ESCB and the European central bank will constitute such a pole.

European Central Bank

There is much work being done and to be done with a view to fostering economic convergence.

But the future of Europe is being actively prepared in another key area, which is also of direct interest to central bankers. I am now referring to the definition of the technical framework in which the future single monetary policy will be conducted. Central banks play a crucial role in this endeavour, in close cooperation with the European monetary institute (EMI), the entity they jointly set up, in accordance with the Treaty, at the beginning of 1994. Let me add that, in defining this framework, the EMI is simply fulfilling one of the main missions which has been given to it by the Treaty, namely, specifying "the regulatory, organizational and logistical framework necessary for the ESCB to perform its tasks."

This framework comprises two key elements: the future European monetary authority and the future European single currency. As far as the authority (ESCB) is concerned, the main objective consists in ensuring that it will be able to conduct efficiently the single monetary policy, right from the start of stage three. With this aim in mind, the ESCB will need relevant concepts and statistics to analyze developments, appropriate instruments and procedures to transmit necessary impulsions to capital markets, and up to date systems to exchange information and payments within the monetary union.

National central banks and the EMI are working intensively on all those topics in order to proceed, in due course, with the necessary adaptations and harmonizations. I must say that the various stances adopted during our discussions are generally closer than might have been expected. Progress is therefore satisfactory and preparations are broadly on schedule. In that respect, I would like to stress that these adaptations and harmonizations will take due account of the subsidiarity principle. It is clear that, for monetary policy, coordination between separate entities is simply not enough. Monetary policy decision-making must be centralised. In the monetary union, monetary policy will be decided by the ECBs Governing Council, the collegial body comprising the governors of the national central banks and the ECBs directors.

But the Treaty itself stipulates that, whenever possible, the implementation of monetary policy decisions will be the responsibility of national central banks. The Treaty thus recognises the crucial role national central banks must play in the future monetary union. Indeed, national central banks are part of each country's national identity; they have an intimate knowledge of the idiosyncrasies of each national financial market (and these idiosyncrasies will not totally disappear with the ongoing harmonization process). In addition, national central banks supervise the development of each financial centre. And the future, as well as the prosperity of Europe hinge critically on the dynamism and competitiveness of its constellation of financial centres.

The second aspect of the preparation of the technical framework is, of course, the preparation of the future single currency. This issue is a complex one because it involves a minimum degree of coordination in the actions of a considerable number of economic agents. This is the reason why the authorities which are currently studying this matter, in particular the EMI at the European level, have engaged wide-ranging consultations with the banking sector and with other future users of the single currency in its various forms. No formal decision has yet been taken but three basic principles seem to stand out:

• First, whatever the date of entry into Monetary Union (in any case, at the latest in January, 1999), it will not be possible to have the single currency fulfill all the traditional functions and take all the forms of a currency, from the beginning. In other words, there will be no complete "big bang" at the outset of Stage three. For instance, ECU denominated notes will probably not be available, due to technical constraints, for three years after the beginning of the monetary union.

• Second, it is generally considered that this period before the introduction of ECU-denominated cash will allow for a better and smoother transition for individuals. We will take into account the constraints of our citizens and we will adopt the best solution for them.

• Third, we cannot enter into monetary union and the irrevocable fixing of the parities of the national currencies concerned with no single currency at all. This would be contrary to the interests of the business community, and, especially, to the interests of those economic agents already largely engaged in cross-border or financial market transactions; these are indeed the transactions which will benefit most directly from the economies of scale generated by the single currency. It is therefore possible to conduct the single monetary policy in the single currency at the very beginning of stage three, and to organize a quick switchover of capital markets to the single currency.

Pragmatic Approach

In conclusion, the Maastricht Treaty on European Union has defined a pragmatic approach to the necessary objective of monetary union:

• First, the Treaty provides for a staged process. Meeting the convergence criteria will require efforts, of course, but nobody believes that, without EMU, European countries could eschew fiscal consolidation.

• Second, the Treaty calls for the decision by heads of state and governments on the entry into the monetary union to be taken before the end of 1996, as the earliest possible date, and states that monetary union starts effectively, in any case, on January 1, 1999. If we take into account the necessary timespan of around twelve months for the active preparation of monetary union after the decision by the European Council is made, this means that the first round of decisions will be completed before the end of 1996 and that the second round is likely to be completed by the end of 1997.

• Third, the Treaty provides for flexibility as regards the dates of entry of the various countries into the monetary union, after the first group of countries starts that union at the latest on January 1, 1999. It is worth noting here that the usual quarrel over whether or not a multi-speed Europe is appropriate, has been solved in the Maastricht Treaty.

It is very important that the Treaty adopted such a pragmatic approach. Indeed, this approach was necessary to ensure that the monetary union will be based on the principle of price stability, to foster growth and job creation. It will also prevent the presence of countries which are not yet ready to join. Last, but not least, this approach will make it possible for monetary union to exist soon enough to stimulate efforts in favour of convergence by the countries which will join later. The whole history of European integration demonstrates the validity of this kind of approach.

Conclusion

Finally, let me just underline three points which I feel are crucial with regards to the monetary construction of Europe. First, Europe has based its future monetary organisation on the principle that monetary credibility and solidity are the best foundations for growth, job creation and prosperity in the European economy. I have the feeling that this founding principle, which is closely adhered to by the Monetary Policy Council of the Banque de France, is also shared by all my European colleagues.

Second, the European monetary union is not only a major structural reform for Europe. It is also a major structural reform for the international monetary system. Personally, I remain convinced that the prosperity and the stability of the global economy requires as responsible as possible an attitude on the part of all major partners and, in particular, responsible behaviour in terms of national savings levels, fiscal policy and monetary policy. This is consistent in what recent G-7 meetings upheld. I am convinced that European monetary union will make a major contribution to responsible management of the global, multipolar monetary system.

Lastly, I cannot help but observe that the trend towards Central Bank independence is not only a European trend, which is now enshrined in the Maastricht Treaty, but is also very much a global trend apparent across all continents. The close link between, on the one hand, monetary credibility, which is necessary in order to benefit from the best financing terms available on the market, and, on the other hand, central bank independence no longer needs to be demonstrated. I know this issue is being debated currently in London. Let me just say how pleased I am that the public debate in my own country provided an opportunity to reassert that Central Bank independence is now an integral part of the French institutional framework.

FOR MONARCHY & SINGLE EUROPEAN CURRENCY.

British Political Traditions Will Endure
Under a New Economic Order

Interview with:	Sir Samuel Brittan,
	Assistant Editor
	Financial Times of London
Directed by:	Tihomir Mikulic and
	William B.Z. Vukson

Margaret Thatcher

Reflecting back to the reign of Margaret Thatcher as Prime-Minister, how has the UK mostly benefitted by her methods of governing?

It may be easier to qualitatively appreciate the benefits from this period than what the statistics represent to be the case. Prior to Margaret Thatcher, we were really in the grip of trade union Barons. This meant that we had a lot of unemployment although most of the unemployed showed up for work. Many restrictive practices were implemented by labour unions and management was afraid to manage. Worst of all, we had a tiny union (the National Union of Mineworkers) in a tiny industry, led by an agitator (Arthur Scargill) that brought down two successive Conservative governments. That was about enough. It also looked as though he would bring down the Thatcher government early on in its tenure, however, hers was the first to stand its ground and rally the police force to enable miners that wanted to work to safely go to work, and ensure that coal was delivered. In retrospect, the action was regarded by all statesmanlike people as provocative, but in fact had worked quite well.

Something similar had also happened in my own industry with several newspaper proprietors exhibiting the courage to face down very strong print unions. Newspaper print unions at that time were used to obstructing any modern developments in the production process. In particular, they became very well known for something called Spanish practices. This meant that unions would insist on being paid for wrapping newspapers which were already wrapped by machinery. It also meant that there were constant stoppages where one never knew whether next morning's newspaper would at all appear. All of these practices came to an end under the Thatcher government.

Contrary to the common view, public spending was not cut very much and the tax burden actually rose, since the public sector deficit was kept down. There was also a small reduction in the dependency culture. It became less easy to draw benefit while not attempting to obtain work. I think that all of these were quite great achievements.

In retrospect, how damaging was the speculative bubble that was built up under Thatcher during the latter part of the 1980s?

It looked very damaging just afterwards in the early 1990s, but compare the outcome with what has materialised in Japan. One can say that the effect was a minnow in the UK.

Did Margaret Thatcher harm the Monarchy?

There was no more of a supporter of the Monarchy than Margaret Thatcher. The truth of the matter is that she is not a radical in any true sense, although her actions are often construed as being so. She never liked to hear anyone ridiculing the Royal family. It was more a coincidence that we had both a queen and the first woman Prime-Minister. There was a feeling around mainly fueled by the media, that the queen did not approve of all of Margaret Thatchers attitudes.

The Monarchy has always traditionally stood to unify the country. It tends to stick up for people very different from themselves, who they believe may have in some way been left out of the ruling establishment. For instance, they had great sympathy for the miners which was very romantic and out of date, but nonetheless very much there at the time.

A Lasting Monarchy

Is Elizabeth II the last ruling monarch in the UK?

My first reaction to that is that there is no such luck. I cannot stand the hypocrisy that circles the Royal family, often disguised as criticism. The obsession with one family, as if they either were or ought to be miraculous if only they can behave better, is offensive to me as a rational being.

Equally, I can see the disadvantages of having an elected President. For instance, you could never have a situation of having an elected mayor of a city not being acceptable to a particular President, because in the UK, the queen does not take part in politics. She is very much advised by her private Secretary of what the constitutional precedents are. Basically, her guiding principle is not to get involved in politics. Very few Presidents can behave this way, and you can not really expect them to, because even the most respected Presidents have usually got a career in party politics behind them.

In your view, what is the prime reason for preserving the institution of the Monarchy?

There is an advantage in having someone that is above politics and is a point of continuity between governments. There are duties for a President to perform. In Italy, for example, a President is sometimes not regarded as being entirely above the battle.

What is the big disadvantage of the Royal family to the UK?

It certainly is not a disadvantage to the economy, as it draws in substantial tourist dollars. However, the disadvantage of it is that it tends to divert attention from the more difficult and perhaps less glamorous issues in the UK. It is much easier to discuss the affairs of Diana and Charles, than to discuss the discount rate policy of the Bank of England.

Bankers to the Queen

What has been the link between the Monarchy and the collapse of Barings bank? Has not the queen been forced to open up castles and various monuments to tourists after Barings occurred?

The Monarchy was not much affected by the collapse of Barings, since most of the assets of the Royal family are in shares, trusts or land. They really only keep petty cash in the bank. In any case, the assumption of Barings by Dutch based ING bank, has preserved all of Barings former deposits. There is no reason to believe that the Royal family had a major proportion of its assets managed by Barings at all.

I may be wrong, but I cannot think of any additional Royal residences that were opened to the public as a result of the Barings crisis. The opening of Buckingham Palace to tourists began well before the Barings crisis.

I do not understand how Nick Leeson was able to acquire such uncontested powers to destroy a bank?

The analogy would be one where you had an individual not academically talented, but one that had great ability in making money, nonetheless. It would be most tempting to give him a great deal of independence. Before the crash, they were reporting profits from this one individual in Singapore that were greater than in all other activities in which Barings was engaged in. In the end, he was not doing anything that complicated; he was simply betting on the Tokyo Stock Exchange.

The Bank of England

In a period of independent central banking, why has the UK not followed suit with the overall European trend?

Mainly because of the confrontation between the two main political parties. According to the mythology, the government is responsible for everything that happens. John Major is terrified that somebody will criticise him over the direction of interest rates and he will have no choice but to respond: "I can't do anything about it." I favour central bank independence myself, but its probably easier for a country with a written constitution after World War II like Germany, to write out formally.

Has the lack of central bank independence affected the value of sterling on the foreign exchange markets?

It's difficult to relate the value to events that have not taken place. However, having said that, if an announcement were made that the Bank of England were to be independent, or not subject to a directive of the Chancellor over monetary policy, I think that bonds and sterling would go up and would go up even more if the Labour party were to proclaim full support for such a move and refrain from any policy reversals.

Contemporary Issues of Concern

How do you view George Soros speculative power that was attributed to plunging sterling out of the European Exchange Rate Mechanism (ERM) in 1992?

It was not at all Soros on his own. He saw the way the wind was blowing and made some very wise investments accordingly. He did not, however, cause the wind to blow. In retrospect, when the UK joined, it had no idea that the German interest rate would stay so high for so long. At the time, there was some support in the UK treasury for a general re-alignment in the ERM, which also would have involved France, which was not prepared to have a depreciation against the mark, since they were already focusing their sights on monetary union.

How do you respond to the constant criticism that the UK has hardly a manufacturing base left?

I do not lose any sleep over it at all. In the 18th century there were a group of economists known as the Physiocrats that thought that agriculture was the most important activity. The ones that talk about manufacturing currently, belong in a similar category. Manufacturing is just one sector in the economy and activity has been moving away from manufacturing in many advanced economies quite recently. The whole process seems pretty natural to me.

Is it not the UKs unofficial policy to de-face what is left of its industrial base?

It is not a policy, but can be more accurately described as allowing the natural course to run and just letting things happen. The US has a far smaller proportion of its population in manufacturing than does the UK. If we look at a trend of Gross National Product (GNP) per head in a given country, what we will find is that the higher the GNP per head; the smaller is the proportion of the economy in manufacturing. The UK is exactly on this trend, but Germany is very much off of trend, which may make it a bit vulnerable as change takes place.

Policy Suggestions

What in particular excites you about the UK economy at this moment?

If you asked me what could excite me? I would respond by saying that I do not think that economies are unique. For the first time, we seem to be combining reasonable growth, falling unemployment and no visible inflation pressures. It seems to be the first time in about thirty years that we have developed such a positive combination of macro-economic aggregates.

Although UK GNP is rising, it is rising very slowly. I think there are two reasons for that, one is that markets on continental Europe are very sluggish and that statistics under rate GNP growth rates. For instance, the effect of information technology has not been fully captured by the numbers.

If you could change one thing in the UK economy in a real sense, what would it be?

I would try to abolish the standard wage that exists across an entire class of jobs. For example, there is currently a big shortage of science teachers, however, a surplus exists in the field of art instruction. It would be very much against popular culture to allow schools to pay more for science instructors.

Also, a great divergence exists between insiders and outsiders. Those that have jobs try to keep up their wage at the expense of outsiders, who are prepared to work for a lower pay. One way around this would be for firms to hire outsiders at a lower wage. In other words, I would like to rid the UK of the fixed wage construct.

Do you favour a Labour government under Tony Blair, or would you like to see an extension of the tenure of the Conservatives?

One party has been in office for far too long, but I would prefer a change based on economic policy. I find that these Conservative politicians are rather tired people and appeal to all of the worst instincts to hang on to power.

Will sterling become a part of a single European currency soon?

I do not think it will be among the inner group of participants. I think that it is very likely that the government will like to join later on, which has been our story with relations to Europe since World War II.

Is Germany importing many UK financial practices at this time?

Paradoxically, Germany has a very admirable record with its monetary policy, but a very poor record in business. One disadvantage of the German corporate model is that there exists only one point of pressure to conform- and that is from the banks, which is not always enough. It may not be a bad thing if there were to be some fear of a takeover of a German firm.

Do you not think that the German culture of production and exports would find it hard to adapt to the new changing environment among all industrial economies?

Yes, the German model is in great trouble. German companies are exporting investment to countries where labour costs are much less.

Would not the UK's participation in a single European currency somewhat strain its historical trans-Atlantic commercial relations?

Only to those business people who have always been opposed to a single European currency for the UK from the very beginning.

Are there more business people against, as opposed to being in favour of a single currency?

Not in the manufacturing sector, which still composes some 20 to 25 percent of GNP in the UK and composes more than one-half of all exports, even though I referred to its relative unimportance earlier on. Moreover, the biggest opposition exists in the City of London, as opposed to the general overall business community in the UK. The attitude in the City is based more on their political orientation than it is on their commercial interests.

What would have to happen for the UK to accept a single currency?

Either something very good or something very bad. If the single currency is working, then a Blair government may opt to join immediately. The other event that may cause Britain to change its mind would be yet another sterling crisis. After which the prevailing sentiment which may emerge, would be one that questions our ability to solve our problems through devaluation yet again? Faced with a choice of devaluation, yet again, and raising interest rates to punitive levels, and joining a single currency, the latter option may emerge as the least worst of the three evils. Therefore, we would need to have a climate where the single currency is shown to be working, or a sterling disaster is in the works, or some sort of combination of these two events.

ONE MARKET ONE MONEY?

Interview with: **Paul DeGrauwe,**
                      Member of the Belgian Senate
                      & Advisor on European Monetary Union

Directed by: **William B.Z. Vukson**

What do you expect from the 1996 Maastricht constitutional conference?

It is becoming clearer that the present strategy towards monetary union simply will not work. There exists just too much turbulence in the currency markets at this time, in order to pursue the framework as was envisioned in the Maastricht Treaty towards European monetary union (single currency).

Specifically, what is the strategy that must be changed?

The present strategy calls for a long time period in order to reach the ultimate goal of monetary union, together with economic "convergence conditions" on a number of economic variables such as deficits, debts, inflation and long term interest rates among a majority of European countries, which are basically irrelevant to monetary union. In fact, economic convergence can only come after a successful introduction of a single currency, which is the opposite to the strategy that is presently being followed by European governments. In that respect, one of the visions that must be addressed is the softening of this criteria.

Would this also call for a complete revision in the current role of the European Exchange Rate Mechanism (ERM)?

The ERM must be revised completely, especially within the current mood of speculative pressures in the currency markets. Moreover, the turbulence witnessed presently should become even more pronounced as the final date of 1999, inscribed in the Maastricht Treaty approaches. Why is that? One fundamental reason is that a guessing game of what country will be in or out is continually on the minds of investors, and world money markets just cannot cope with this kind of uncertainty. The solution will either shorten the transition period significantly, or allow maximum flexibility in our managed system of exchange rates.

What would you propose to be the correct road to monetary union in Europe?
First, it would not be a good idea to attempt a monetary union with the entire European Union as it presently stands with 15 members. The reason being that many member states are still very different structurally and institutionally, such

that they have to maintain as an option, flexible exchange rates to correct any imbalances that affect their economies. Having said that, how do we then select those that should be in? The criteria should be based on the individual countries themselves- they are the ones that would know if monetary union would be in their best interests.

Regardless of their economic fundamentals?

No, but the current criteria that has been imposed touching on such concerns as debts and deficits is not the right way to go either. This scientific approach to European monetary union as per the Maastricht Treaty has gone too far. Many of the criteria, such as the one on inflation convergence are completely irrelevant. For example, when east and west Germany were united, no one referred to inflation differences, yet the monetary union is holding to this day rather successfully.

Why has the Maastricht criteria been introduced?

The Germans imposed this on the entire European Union to restrict access for the southern members, such as Portugal, Spain, Italy and Greece, due to their distrust of their economic management skills.

Stated differently, if there is a single currency for the European Union, it can only be the Deutsche mark?

Yes, since the Bundesbank has displayed a successful track record of financial management since the second World War. Nonetheless, I believe monetary union in Europe will be a very difficult idea to successfully implement if the Germans insist on imposing their terms.

In essence, the entire program depends on Germany, which is why I am relatively pessimistic because my reading is that the opposition within Germany will only increase to monetary union. The German government will continue to insist on the rigid implementation of the strict convergence criteria as per the Maastricht Treaty. Since monetary union in Europe means throwing away the German mark.

Is the French economy fundamentally different from the German?

All European economies are different, but the question is whether these differences will be an obstacle to monetary union? I believe that structural differences should not be obstacles to monetary union.

Even at the expense of greater long-term unemployment in France?

I would not attribute the current unemployment problems in France on issues concerning monetary policy. They are a direct result from policies introduced by the Socialist government elected in the early 1980s, such as minimum wages, large increases in social security costs, and so on. However, I would agree with you that restrictive monetary policies practised thus far in the 1990s, have added to the overall problem of unemployment needlessly. Much of the problem was imported by overly restrictive policies in Germany which the French slavishly followed and which intensified the recession in France.

Would you agree that the active pursuit of restrictive monetary policy over the past 14 years, together with the movement making central banks independent or unaccountable to the political process has contributed to the current problem of demand deficiency in industrialised countries?

I'm not so sure that central bank deflation is the major cause of the current deflationary climate, but I would argue that it has been caused in the way in which the ERM has functioned. For example, in the recession of 1991 to 1993, the German Bundesbank pursued an objective of low inflation, countering the price pressures which arose from German re-unification.

However, France did not have this problem, but was forced due to its commitment to a relatively fixed exchange rate within the ERM to maintain a fixed parity to the Deutsche mark, as the mark began to appreciate. Therefore, it was more an issue centred around the willingness of the French political authorities to maintain a relatively fixed parity with an appreciating mark, than it is with regards to the independence of the Bank of France. It would have been far wiser for French policy-makers to allow the franc to float during this period of severe imbalances in the German domestic economy.

Do you agree that inflation must exist in a market economy for it to function effectively?

Yes, it could be a valid objective to pursue. The recent experience with respect to the pursuit of monetary policy from 1991 to 1993 was a repeat of the errors that the US Federal Reserve made during the years of the 1930s great depression. When the depression began, the Federal Reserve restricted money and credit formation, when indeed the opposite should have occurred. This entire episode was repeated in the 1990s in Europe. Germany convinced most European Union members that inflation was about the only important policy goal to be concerned with.

Can it be viewed as a unique scenario that built up as a direct result of the European Union's pre-occupation with monetary union?

Yes, I believe so.

European Financial Architecture

If it is decided at the 1996 Maastricht constitutional conference that a single currency ought to be pursued, how must the banking system prepare for it?

I think that transitional problems will exist, but it really should not change too much. The inter-bank market will grow dramatically, since all national whole-sale credit markets will become one larger European based market, with lower transactions costs and perhaps with cheaper credit over the long term.

Which financial centre will prosper under a single currency: London, Frankfurt or Paris?

It will depend much on the regulatory environment. In the recent past, London was open and Frankfurt very heavily regulated. If a single currency comes about and regulations become standardised, those not participating in the single currency project may end up the losers. If the UK exercises its opt-out clause, it will lose ground to both Frankfurt and Paris.

Will London not be the loser anyway, since regulatory standardisation across all financial centres in the European Union will result in its losing this advantage that it has always held claim to?

Yes, but London does have a unique access and availability of financial talent that is very unique to the three financial centres. From this perspective, London may become even more attractive in a monetary union. Even though the European central bank will be located in Frankfurt, there is no guarantee that Frankfurt will become the major financial centre in Europe. We can only look to the US, where New York is the major financial centre, but Washington D.C. is where the major financial policy decisions are made.

What is the attraction of Paris as the main financial centre?

I see very few attractions to Paris as a financial centre. If the UK participates in a single European currency, there is no question of London remaining the pre-eminent financial centre. If the UK stays out, the issue becomes one of who takes over? This is very difficult to predict at this time.

Will a single currency help to develop a unified retail banking system across Europe?

It will all depend on the regulatory framework in the individual countries, more so than through the actual presence of a single currency circulating in the economy. If we look at the US example once again, a single currency and common monetary policy did not prevent the development of one of the most segmented banking systems in the world at the state level, regardless of the circulation of a common dollar.

Will Belgium, Sweden & Italy default on their debts?

I don't believe so.

Will it not be harder for them to participate in a monetary union?

I don't believe that debt levels have anything to do when making such a determination. If a single currency comes about, debts will be denominated in the same currency, but will still be identified with their respective government borrowers such as Italy, Germany, Belgium and so on. However, now there will not exist a currency risk component priced into the bonds, and each government bond will be rated based on the risk of default. For example, an Italian government ECU-denominated bond may be rated (BBB), whereas the German government ECU-denominated bonds will be rated (AAA) and so on. Each government will have only a risk premium priced according to its default potential reflected through its rating and interest rates. Why would this not be workable?

Do you foresee an acceleration in currency crises as we approach the Maastricht constitutional conference in 1996?

I foresee multiple currency crises up to the year 2000. The only way to avoid these at this point in time is to shorten the transition period to a single currency, because this transition period itself encourages speculation. The entire reason for speculative attacks in the currency markets centres around credibility issues at this very moment.

BUSINESS AND THE ECONOMY UNDER PRESSURE

Old economy sectors made way for the internet and high tech venture capital financing, as old-guard commercial banks struggled to find a way to lend money to the industries of the "new economy." Not only were business relations changing rapidly, but the role of governments was as well, as members of the G7 were forced to address spiralling deficits and debts in the early to the middle part of the decade.

In "Accounting Houses," Sami Helewa uses humour in his title to depict the uni-dimensional stand in which governments have been devoting most of their time to addressing their fiscal finances. According to him, governments ought to have been addressing more substantive concerns such as poverty, healthcare and economic development of small and medium sized enterpris-

es. *The critique is directed to the slow changes in bank credit policies that were not quick enough in realising that we are no longer operating within the realm of the "old economy."*

"Flying Wings Through Hard Times," is a direct critique of airline deregulation in the U.S., which is bound to spread into the European and Asian spheres. As demand for air travel increases, the congestion at airports and airspace render this form of transportation more and more dangerous with the passage of time. Already, many U.S. airlines are continuously operating under Chapter 11 bankruptcy, while those that remain profitable are forced to cut back on services and inconvenience passengers via the "hub-and-spoke" system of operation. Clearly, there must be a call for structural change in the provision of air travel services in order to address the countless operating issues that face the travelling public.

"Canada Watch" is an article that was written at the height of the fiscal crisis in Canada. It was about Canada's attempts to address the fiscal mess that its finances were in, but was unique to the experiences of most G7 members. As the economy changed from a manufacturing base to a service-based economy, it became easier to collect revenues which were dependent on volume and turnover, particularly within the financial services sector. This, combined with growth in the latter years led to unprecedented budget surpluses throughout the G7, providing a basis for lower interest rates in the future.

W.b.z.V.

ACCOUNTING HOUSES

Financial leadership misguides government social policies in Canada and the United States and undermines the efficiency of their democracies

Sami Helewa S.J.

To write for a purpose is beyond the call of duty. To understand the truth is very challenging. To fight for the truth is a vocation worth having. To reflect on and improve one's own surroundings is a life worth living. To imagine a better world sets a tone for new thinking. I am a believer that truth shared is a noble one for we cannot reach maturity without it. Noble truth and its morality command us to make sense of today's global public finance picture, and encourages a voice against its detrimental effects on humanity and capital distribution.

Finance and politics are inseparable. At least the Keynesian economic philosophy links both out of necessity. This necessity has had a historical significance since the Great Depression of the 1920s and 1930s. Governmental involvement in the domestic economy, ensured a world of economic regulation, resource allocation, capital distribution and civility of economic values. Such values encompass elderly pensions, public health care, unemployment compensation, welfare assistance and a sense of governmental fostering towards the less fortunate. The essence of public finance is to ensure a sense of economic fairness, far from the status quo of the French before their Revolution in 1789. This was a Revolution which should still speak loud to all in power, whether in government or in financial institutions.

Recently, the world had two political polars of capitalism and communism, the West struggled to show to its counterpart that economic capitalism supercedes the communist one. The West proved to be right in its conviction, and its triumph crystalised, once the Soviet Union became no more. However, the West shortly afterwards, gradually abandoned its commitment to its domestic economy, as if the former communists became the only ones to impress. This is a grave error that the capitalist West is committing to. Allow me to illustrate.

Technology, a Key Counter-balance

What broke the Soviet Union is technological advancement, which was the main competitive edge between East and West. The Apollo missions onto the moon mirrored the technological competition between the United States and the former Soviet Union, during the Cold War. One aspect of technology which improved a lot in the last decade, and within the last stages of the Cold War era was communications. A touch tone effort links different corners of this globe. The former Soviet Union, with its strict regulation in virtually all aspects of its domestic economy, failed to restrain the tele-communications advancement from the West. News from outside the former Soviet Union became essentially an invasion to the sovereignty of the entire Union. The shut-in policy of the Soviet Union came to an end, causing a new wave of trade liberalisation and setting up free trade zones across the globe. All this happened in a span of less than ten years; the speed of political and economic developments are unprecedented in modern history.

The myth of technology is its contribution to the well-being of our lifestyle. In fact, at the work place an employee receives facsimile material which it expects a prompt answer due to the availability of advanced telecommunications. Previously, the manner of business communications was largely through mail, which did not encourage an immediate response. Due to the rapidity of tele-communications, it has affected ways of human thinking and lifestyles of prompt action. The rapidity of current social policy development, for example, reflects the cultural aspect of today's tele-communications.

Free trade zones were created in a short span of time and within the two US presidential terms of George Bush and Bill Clinton. The Free Trade Agreement (FTA) between Canada and the United States was immediately followed by Nafta, then Apec, meanwhile there were the struggles of the European Union to ensure, rather desperately, a single common currency on the continent. A balanced budget for the US within a seven year period is another example, after a consistent deficit since the Korean War. All of these swift political developments are in essence, aspects of the new culture of tele-communications and technological advancement.

Sadly, the culture of tele-communications-rapidity style has invaded the governmental milieu. Quick decisions are considered signs of strength, regardless of ramifications. A balanced budget in the short term is the religion of any government in their policy-ritual-making these days. The outcomes of massive unemployment and cuts on welfare recipients, are no longer political issues, as long as a balanced budget takes precedence. Once again, these new wave governmental policies reflect the status quo of our technological economy, abandoning the social aspects and ramifications of public finance.

The Excellence of Banking

As 1995 was ending, the chartered banks in Canada started to disclose their financial statements. Record profits were the highlights in the media and the interpretation of the profit figures, gave the chartered banks the reputation of fine financial pillars within a weak economy. Of course, such news pleases few and angers a larger audience. Bank employees' salaries are almost frozen on average, and declining full-time employment benefits speak louder to the contribution of these profits.

In addition, the "no risk" underwriting procedures of their credit policy towards small and medium size enterprises, render these banks to questionable ability in assessing a good risk. To assume no risk on enterprises of potential long term employment, in my opinion, is not a banking skill. To operate a banking system largely on higher service fees, and as a result, declare profits, is by no means one of the finest banking moments! In fact, it shows the lack of commitment these institutions have displayed towards the Canadian economy. It is disgusting to say the least.

Banks should have some degree of moral obligations towards employment creation in such a difficult economy, which is continuously substituting labour for computer services. Having said that, Canadian banks should specialise in

assessing risks associated with the small and medium sized business sector, as
opposed to generalising such risks as threats to their lending policy. If most of
the job creation in today's economy comes in smaller firms, then the banks
must get realistic about these firm's liquidity needs.

Leadership without Leadership

A pull-out from the economy in the manner that banks in Canada have so far
undertaken, seems to have an effect on both the federal and provincial governments. Sadly and likewise, at this moment, governments also show strong
intentions to pull out from the economy. This has been one of the greatest
sources of instability for this nation to sustain.

This trend of governmental pull out is not only a Canadian phenomenon. The
United States is likewise on the same trend. After a massive deficit and ever
enlarging public debt during the Reagan administration, the 1990s are hit with
a reversal trend in the form of budget cuts in expenditures. In fact, the deficit
has become the sole excuse against the funding of governmental social programs. The Speaker of the House, Newt Gingrich, the ever popular politician
made a name for himself due to his social program cuts against single-parent
subsidies. However, the US budget deficit cuts are immune from military
expenditures, but social programs do not have similar privileges!

In Ontario, we have Premier Mike Harris and his incredible cuts affecting the
poor of his province to the point that I anticipate an increase in activities of
organised crime and prostitution in the major cities. A government ought not to
pull out from an economy for the sake of balancing their books of expenditure.
What does it mean to have a balanced budget? Under what conditions do we
need to have such a financial balance? Are there not certain conditions for a
government to pursue such a goal? Does it make sense to cut governmental
programs at a time of economic depression? If yes, then why do we need to
have a government at all? Why and what is the use of a government which is
elected to cause further uncertainty in the economies of its district? Many questions with no answers of average reason!

Once again, I ask, what is the meaning of a balanced budget? Why now, is
another significant question our politicians in Canada and the US should
answer? When previous minister of finance Michael Wilson under former
Canadian Prime Minister Brian Mulroney, introduced the goods and services
tax (GST), which was a sudden seven percent sales tax increase, he said the
purpose of this tax was simply to ensure similar social programs for future generations. Wilson's point was that the GST was introduced as an alternative to
borrowing against the future. A few years later, both the federal and provincial
governments are instead cutting their social programs, while still collecting
GST revenue.

At a time of technical revolution, which renders much of the labour force worthless in front of computer services and a banking system obsessed with profit making, without a significant contribution to a job-creation economy, the governments do the same for the sake of balancing their books. Since when does a government ought to have a balanced budget? A government in situations of economic depression has a moral obligation to maintain a budget deficit; this is no exaggeration in relation to what a balanced budget actually costs: considering that the cuts are on programs the less fortunate depend upon, a wider gap between the upper classes and the poor is certain. An imbalance of capital distribution is another cost with adverse eschatological effects of social unrest, if not a revolution similar to the French Revolution, over two hundred years ago and the current one being played out. Must a government pursue a balanced budget during these hard days of massive unemployment? The answer is clearly no, no and no. What sort of governmental leadership is it that follows the philosophy of the banking system? Assumed leadership is not the same as authentic leadership.

In democracy, a government is put to power by its people to serve them. Service should not encompass a letdown in reducing their social programs as a means to set their accounting books straight. A budget deficit is unfortunate, but a balanced budget ought not to be socially costly. Reason alone, does not justify governmental pull-out from the domestic economy during times of economic recession.

I find it hard to accept that Newt Gingrich was selected to be the man of the year; it is so sad that *Time Magazine* could not find a more suitable candidate. During the great depression of the 1930s, the fictitious characters of Superman and later Walt Disney's Mickey Mouse played roles of moral justice in films and cartoons. Perhaps in our current times, we can learn and be inspired by them, as economic justice gradually fades from public finance.

INITIAL INVESTIGATION: FLYING WINGS THROUGH HARD TIMES

Deregulation in US aviation inflicted unprecedented harm to the industry and provided a warning for those on the threshold of deregulation

Sami E. Helewa S.J.

Aviation remains one of the wonders of this century. The advancements achieved in technology and innovation have pulled pairs of wings well above the surface. It all started as an experiment against forces of gravity, as flying techniques advanced to pull aircraft from departure points to specific destinations.

It did not take long for air mail services in the United States to become a viable business in the first quarter of this century. Later, airlines were incorporated and became a major fixture of the domestic transportation industry. What took great travellers like Marco Polo, Christopher Colombus, Thomas Cook and Ibn Battuta to cover large distances, is covered today in a few hours. The supremacy of the present speaks loudly over its inferior past.

Behind the engineering excellence of aircraft manufacturing is another world of policy making, regulation, deregulation, competition and airline safety to name a few. During the Carter Administration, the US Airline Industry was legally deregulated after years of debate between Congress, airline boards of directors and aviation agencies.

The aftermath of deregulation opened a new chapter of intense competition, new airline routes and new airline entrants into the industry. Deregulation took its toll mainly on ticket prices, a very controversial factor of its influence on airline safety, which remained subject to regulation.

However, airline safety in the recent past has become a larger concern. Deregulation is blamed for the lower safety standard many airlines experience, even though safety remained under the grip of regulation! So why has it become a national issue during deregulation? Safety is an ambiguous and relative term to the American public. It is strongly associated with the absence of airline disasters as opposed to the maintenance and provision of a safe sky zone for aircraft.

In fact there is no unanimously agreeable definition of airline safety with the American public; citizens are mostly automobile owners and they are more in tune with car safety than airline safety. Despite the fact that automobile safety is by far less complex than its cousin, the aircraft. Sole ownership of a vehicle plays a major role in the awareness of vehicle safety.

In the case of airlines, owners are either stock owners (not all airlines are privatised), governments or both. For them, safety remains a given factor, as long as there are no airline disasters, as opposed to the profit potential an aircraft may yield. Besides, a passenger whose confidence in today's technology surpasses safety doubts, pushes safety to the secondary realm as well. Hence, technological expectations quite often supersede all safety considerations by the public. For instance, NASA's Challenger disaster in January, 1986 was a crying signal against sole association of safety to technological advancement.

In reality technology does not warrant safety, even though new aircraft are sophisticated. Safety remains largely a matter of precaution measurement expected from and enforced on an airline to minimise or eliminate at best, any chance of aircraft accidents. The intake of such a goal is the combination of existing technology and acquired skills, as requested to cope with the advancement of aircraft technology.

What Was Achieved Under Deregulation?

Prior to the inception of deregulation, the airline industry grew with the increased demand for its services and flying became the most frequent way of travelling through long distances. The need for new routes, especially for shorter distances, became a pressing concern since the regulation of airlines prevented new entrants and access to new routes.

As deregulation gained its political momentum and debates were opened, the general economic philosophy for deregulation was perfect competition. This was in an academic sense, the sign of the times to abandon the Keynesian philosophy of interfering in sectors of the economy. The rules of the laissez-faire (unregulated) market meant open markets for competition and new airline routes for the aviation industry.

Consequently, competition increased as the number of entrants escalated. Since 1978, the year that deregulation became official, an estimated 150 new airlines entered into the competitive game, of which 118 declared bankruptcy or merged with other carriers. Some of the well established names like PAN AM and TWA struggled to survive. The airline sector turned out to be the first obvious casualty from adopting the perfect competition model in conducting their business, a fact often denied by the remaining advocates of the free market mechanism.

The most significant effect of deregulation is the ticket price reduction. The price war among carriers has transformed airline competition, based on quality of services and travel comfort of the pre-deregulation era, to the current price competition. In essence that was one primary goal of deregulation. Passengers gained from the whole ordeal of deregulation as the average ticket price became 40 percent cheaper.

However, nothing comes free. With the price war, passengers had to accept the hub and spoke system. This prolonged their travelling time, since they had to land via an intermediary airport to load additional passengers, prior to their final destination. The passengers' gain from the price reduction, is offset by the inconvenience inflicted by the hub and spoke system.

When US airlines began to feel the crunch of the price war on their flying operation and began to record successive losses, to avoid the likelihood of bankruptcy, mergers were often the only alternative. When you have an industry experiencing a sudden foreign acquisition, or semi-acquisition (British Airways and USAir, for example), it is usually a sign of a troubled industry.

The financial troubles are self-inflicted, since price wars have one primary purpose: to cut the throats of other carriers in order to achieve a higher market share. A case which does not reflect the genuine goal of an airline in offering a quality service. The price war produced the alternative of a cheap travelling service, as opposed to the quality that the industry had offered prior to the inception of deregulation.

The logic offered by the advocates of deregulation or the free market mechanism, was simply that business travellers with higher ticket prices, would increase to the point of subsidising the much lower ticket prices offered to the economy class. Such myopic vision naturally did not foresee that the advancement in telecommunications has had much impact in reducing business travelling, to a point in which an airline could no longer count on this premium.

Why Did Deregulation Not Maintain a High Safety Standard?

Airline safety is costly, since it requires aircraft maintenance in a regular periodical manner by expensive labour. With the price war, the expenditure on maintenance is naturally reduced:

• one result of this was an unprecedented factor in the history of US aviation; aging aircraft. The emergency landing of the Aloha Airlines 737 in Hawaii after it lost its top in 1988- due to metal fatigue- is supportive evidence of its age considering it has been in operation since 1969, a period of 19 years!

• the reduction in maintenance costs is also reflected in the available number of mechanics for each aircraft. TWA, for instance, with an average age of over 14 years in its fleet (an age which warrants higher maintenance) has, instead of increasing its number of mechanics, reduced them by a staggering 20 percent. Such logic in operating an aging fleet has no roots in economic theory, so why have it in reality? A question advocates and academic economists of free competition did not answer for. To put the safety issue in perspective, the only remaining interpretation of the above figures, is that the reduction in maintenance expenditures on the aging fleet, is solely due to the price war permitted under deregulation. The mega losses of $10 billion accumulated since 1989, and thousands of job losses in the aviation industry in the recent past, sadly reiterate the lower safety expenditures.

• the creation of the hub and spoke system which is for the convenience of airlines, has also a negative impact on airline safety. The hub and spoke generates more frequent take offs and landings prior to the final destination. The take offs and landings are considered the most dangerous stages of any flight, and when a passenger wants to go from point A to destination B through C, instead of going directly, this passenger and the airline are doubling their chances of disaster. The effect more than doubles in view of the listed points above!

• the traffic controllers strike during the first year of the Reagan Administration, caused the majority to leave their careers permanently. This was a political gain to Reagan, but not so to aviation, since the quality of these controllers could not be replaced.

• the training requirement for new controllers is no longer as rigorous as it used to be, a fact which is alarming in view of the increased flight congestion generated by the hub and spoke system of operation. The same applies to new pilot recruitment. In 1983, a pilot needed 2,300 hours of flying time plus uncorrected 20/20 vision; now a pilot is required to have only 800 hours and correctable vision is accepted by most airlines!

Conclusion: Any New Directions?

Amid the self-inflicted wounds of airlines in the United States, there are many debates to regulate ticket prices once again and restrict competition to avoid any further losses. The latter as mentioned earlier, are estimated at $10 billion since 1989. Even though such losses force aviation experts and consultants to rethink regulation and re-consider its prospects, it remains more of a desperate reactionary move as opposed to a realistic and politically profound one. Re-regulation will not be a feasible option due to:

• monetary and political costs. President Clinton's intention to raise taxes is for proposed health care reform, which is on the top of his political priority agenda. The monetary cost would eventually and largely lie on American citizens in the form of higher ticket prices. More expensive tickets would induce lower demands for travelling, an event which the financially troubled industry cannot tolerate at this time. In addition, the impact of lower demand would further depress the aircraft manufacturing sector.

• the fact that it is too late to re-regulate. The essence of this argument is large-

ly founded on the financial and political reality abroad. The timing factor is
quite crucial. The European Union (EU), for example, is moving towards de-
regulating its aviation industry and unleashing competition from the grip of
regulation. If this comes into effect, then the United States would gain access
to new routes to the EU, and the already cheaper US tickets would enhance a
financial plus to the ailing US aviation industry.

• existing investment in organisation. Carriers expanded on the ground through
the infra-structure of the hub and spoke, some of which were beyond any economic sense. Not all of them are money making hub and spokes, particularly
those in smaller areas like San Jose and Nashville. To re-regulate these hubs
would not necessarily put them out of operation. In fact, such moves should
entirely come from the airlines which own these hubs.

• burdens on the Federal Budget. The federal government would end up facing
enforced subsidies to the ailing aviation industry, which is eventually an
increased tax proposal. Clinton is most unlikely to pursue this route, since as
mentioned earlier, healthcare is his priority.

If not re-regulation then what? The alternative is to look at the facts and expectations of the status quo. Currently, the potential for new carriers to enter, even
with the open competition, is no longer financially feasible to the industry.
However, the losses associated with re-regulation are likely to be enormous,
since it would involve the restructuring of airlines and airports (further job
losses are likely to occur.)

The hard lesson that the US aviation industry passed on left only a few carriers
to operate. To maintain the de-regulation status quo is a better outcome, since
the industry cannot tolerate additional losses associated with re-regulation.
Besides, with a lot fewer airlines in today's aviation market, the price war is
about to end and the ticket prices would eventually level among carriers.

The burden of any action largely lies on the airlines themselves. Price competition in the way it was introduced caused bankruptcies; so airlines should abandon the illusion that reasonable higher prices would slice off their market share.
Thus, airlines should increase their ticket prices for the purpose of:

• covering costs of their operation (safety should be a fixed cost for their new
aircraft fleet and an increasing variable one for aging aircraft)

• allowing prices to reflect distance travelled. It does not make sense for longer
travelling distances to have lower fares than the shorter ones, as is often the
case presently.

The other part of the adjustment burden lies on the Clinton Administration. The
White House should seriously consider the revision of the existing bankruptcy
law. Under the latter, a carrier facing bankruptcy can still operate and influence

lower market prices for other carriers. Eastern Airlines spent years under Chapter 11 of the bankruptcy law before it went out of business in 1991. Such a revision would allow the surviving carriers to focus on marketing quality flying operations, as opposed to worrying about the price war.

CANADA WATCH: A REPORT ON THE POST BUDGET MOOD

The Finance Minister will reshape the nation's political interrelation between the Federal and Provincial governments as a necessity to control the national debt

Jerry J. Khouri

The Canadian budget has come and gone. By now observers of Canada know what its fiscal direction will look like over the next few years. To recap, Finance Minister Paul Martin Jr. will fundamentally reduce the deficit, currently standing at fiscal year 1994/95 at Cdn. $37.9 billion to $21.3 billion by fiscal year 1996/97. This not only matches the government's objective of three percent of GDP but will surpass it. In fact, according to Nesbitt Burns, one of the voices of the Canadian establishment, it estimates a potential deficit of only $10-13 billion in fiscal year 1997/98.

With the above in mind, the debate on the budget has been elevated since its proclamation at the end of February. Over the past year Canadians or rather, to be more accurate, certain Canadians have persuasively and coherently articulated a policy of concentrating on Canada's deficit and debt. This grouping includes the banking sector, large corporations, the financial press and an assortment of publicly known economists, politicians and investors. At the other corner, there rests social policy activists, Canadian nationalists, labour organizations and its own assortment of publicly known economists, politicians and investors. This group advocates that while the deficit/debt question is notable, the country has lost sight of job creation and social justice.

International readers of this book, may not appreciate fully the changes both in public discourse and policy that Canada currently is experiencing. Canada, according to one argument, cannot maintain the vast array of programs that have existed for years. The fiscal situation simply does not allow the type of spending presently occurring. Hence, the backdrop to the Martin budget. Incidentally, a new book by author Linda McQuaig called *"Shooting the Hippo"* is receiving much attention. The author quotes liberally from a study by a leading statistician at Statistics Canada, that debunks the popular perception that social programs drain the deficit. This study, according to McQuaig, was ignored.

Nevertheless, the finance minister has done what all of his predecessors refused to do. He is cutting spending across the board. Departmental spending (in real dollars) will be cut by 19 percent over the next three years. This will be accompanied by a reduction of 45,000 public service workers. Also, business subsidies will be cut by half and unemployment insurance will be "permanently evaluated" away from dependence towards independence. Privatization and the "commercialization of government services" will be introduced. This includes selling CN Rail, commercial air navigation, and the remaining 70 percent of Petro Canada. Foreign aid is also targeted, an issue that has perturbed the foreign affairs community, in light of the new review of Canadian foreign policy urging a commitment of 0.7 percent of GNP, a goal set by the Group of Seven nations.

All this is exhaustive in relative terms. But what seems to have sparked the most reaction is that Federal-Provincial relations, in terms of transfers of money, will be altered. Not only will actual transfers be reduced, but that the provinces when dealing with areas such as education, health, and welfare may set their own standards. This issue, called bloc funding, while given a codicil (that it must maintain universality) is really transferring all obligations and responsibilities to the provinces. It is here where the fear of a changing Canada enters.

While many Canadians are proud of their social and health-care system, some fear that the Martin Budget will destroy this sacred cow. It is true that both medicare and health-care are under stringent review, not simply in pecuniary terms, but also in terms of policy. In fact a study released in late January concluded that while billions have been spent over the 1980s, Canadians as a whole were not getting sicker. It also noted the need to make the service more efficient and that Canadians must learn the art of preventive medicine, so as to eliminate the visitation of doctors for minor problems. Canada presently spends ten percent of GDP on health-care, and the government is clear in that it desires a reduction in line with nations such as France and Germany that spend between eight to nine percent. All this when realized, will make Canada a totally different place. Whether this is good or bad is too early to tell. But the fact that it will change is indisputable. The decentralization of policy and the provincialization of standards, some fear, will lead to several Canadas. Others point out that Canada is already divided by regions and such policy measures will simply complement this dynamic.

Moreover, critical voices contend that the budget itself missed a great opportunity, in not addressing the relationship between the role of government and its populace. North Americans as a whole have become cynical about governments and their politicians. In the United States, for example, Washington, as the corridor of government, is so despised that the person in power is really irrelevant. Canadians, while paradoxically still regard Prime Minister Jean Chrétien with high esteem, have a derision towards government and those in it. In other words, what Canada is undergoing is an introspection and a redefinition of the role of government. Traditionally, government has been the place where legal, political, social and economic rights were protected. All this is slowly being reconstructed, a debate that will surely linger beyond the end of the decade.

Finally, at time of writing, the nation "awaits" the decision of Moody's Investors Service Inc., described by some as the "powerful New York-based bond rating agency." It was on February 16, a full twelve days before the budget, Moody's warned Canada that it is in danger of losing its rating, both on its domestic debt and foreign currency debt. There was an outcry by nationalists, not dissimilar to the *Wall Street Journal* remonstration in early January, when it classified Canada a third world nation in relation to its debt issue. Today, the issue persists as Moody's is set to preside. Now the focus includes provincial debts, and the Canadian polity is split along the same political demarcations as the budget debates.

OIL POLITICS AND THE MIDDLE EAST AFTER THE GULF WAR

After the run-up in the oil price during the Gulf War, many consumers believed that they have seen the last of the oil peaks. Deep recession and restructuring throughout most of the 1990s had relegated oil to the heap of the "old economy." Soon the automotive sector began to build heavy, high-margin Sport Utility Vehicles (SUVs), which were hardly friendly to the concept of gasoline conservation. At the end of the decade, the price of oil was once again, an issue.

In the interview of petroleum specialist, Atif Kubursi, he gives us a brief glimpse of some rare political moves initiated by the U.S. through their Middle Eastern proxy- Saudi Arabia. The fact that the Gulf War was such a drain on the Saudi surplus, and the fact that the U.S. continues to run very high balance of trade deficits, any oil price movements are always suspect. It is very tempting to ask whether the recent oil price increases in 2000 have anything to do with supply and demand, or whether they were engineered to help the Saudi's with their financial difficulties and to discourage any repatriation of funds or investments out of U.S. dollars.

W.b.z.V.

THE POLITICS OF OIL AND WATER

Interview with:	Atif A. Kubursi
Directed by:	Jerry J. Khouri

During the past couple of years there has been a shift in discourse on the question of "the end of history" and the emergence of a new political order. Whether this premise is correct or not, there is nevertheless a fundamental challenge facing world affairs. Where does the entire question of oil and its importance as an exhaustible source of energy sit amidst all this?

One of the major anomalies of history is that oil is concentrated in very few countries; primarily Arab and the Third World that depend very heavily on only one source of income. Whereas consumption is concentrated in the western industrialized countries of the world that consume an inordinate amount of it, exceeding by far whatever is consumed by other countries. Equally important is the fact that most of these countries are net importers of oil in the sense that their consumption needs far exceed their capacity to satisfy it from domestic production. Such being the case, oil, particularly Middle Eastern Arab oil, has become extremely important because it is abundant in the region. In fact, 66 percent of the world's proven reserves come from the region. From one trillion barrels of oil in proven reserves, upwards of 660 billion come from the region, and more than 250 billion barrels from Saudi Arabia alone. This means that all the additional incremental demand for oil must come from one region and one region only- the Gulf. Therefore, there is very heavy dependence on a strategic, vital, non-substitutable and non-renewable commodity from one region of the world.

This is documented by another serious and important fact that oil from the region is still the cheapest oil in the world. The additional incremental costs of lifting one barrel from the well to the wellhead is still less than ten cents. So any price increase generated a large amount of surplus profit that went to foreign investment after the domestic absorptive capacity of the Gulf States reached its limits. The surpluses have been directed primarily to western capital markets and almost exclusively to the US financial markets. In that respect, it represents a transfer from other importing countries like Germany and Japan, to the United States.

Anyway, oil is not only important for being a commodity, it is also important for being a fundable asset that has been invested very heavily in the US market. Thus we have a double dependency here. On the one hand, a dependency on the commodity and on the other a dependency on the surplus to bridge the gap in the US. Because of the chronic balance of payments deficit that has been experienced for years and the oil surplus funds that has helped to moderate it.

Oil has been good to some international companies and devastating for those who live near the oil fields. We have seen damage to the environment and the ecosystem. In general, there exists a contradiction in interests between producers of oil and consumers of oil. One plan described as the internationalization of oil has been proposed as a palliative. What does this mean? And what are your views on this?

Oil is internationalized in a number of respects. It is internationalized in the sense that it is the largest component of international trade, where ten percent of this trade is in oil. More than 250 billion barrels of oil are traded annually. Also, much of this oil is produced, transported, refined and distributed by international companies. There is no mistake about it, oil is one of the most internationalized commodities in the world.

 Internationalization at the moment, unfortunately, on a de facto basis, means American control of this oil. This control is exercised by talks. The strong historical relationship between the United States and Saudi Arabia- the major oil producer, the producer that has the largest capacity and has kept OPEC afloat by its willingness to vary production, represents a capacity on the part of the United States to influence in a very substantive manner all decisions regarding oil.

Actually, there is strong evidence to suggest that the US for years has influenced decisions about oil. As early as 1972, before oil prices increased, the record is clear that the US was lobbying for higher oil prices. In 1972 Arab Foreign Ministers were meeting in Algiers to discuss joint strategy. James Aitkens, the American Ambassador to Saudi Arabia, went to tell the conferees that the US favoured the doubling in real terms of the oil price. A clear signal to the participants that it was in favour of higher oil prices.

There are indications and circumstantial evidence to suggest that the US was the basic and most important beneficiary of higher oil prices. The US had perceived this vulnerability and this increased dependence on importing oil through commitment and desire to promote conservation. Higher oil prices were consistent with this desire, and the US was all too happy to find an outside body to blame for this higher oil price. Due to the extent that it represents a transformation of financial flow from its major competitors, Japan and Germany, into the hands of Saudi Arabia and the other Gulf states, who were unable to digest the surpluses. This meant, ultimately, that the surpluses were transferred to American markets in exchange for extra purchases of weapons and exports. The US was an important net beneficiary, because it was able to compete better over the long-term, relative to its emerging competitors in Europe and Japan.

In a way then the internationalization of oil flies in the face of the Americanization of oil. If indeed, I am willing to suggest that this Americanization of oil, which was oil from 1973 onward, has increased in the wake of the Gulf War, and the increased dependence of these vulnerable Gulf states on American protection, then I am now less opposed to the internationalization of oil. It is not that I would like it to be wrestled away from the hands of the producers, rather I would like it to be wrestled out of the hands of the exclusive control of the Americans. But the issue is not the internationalization of oil, but the de-Americanization of oil. What one wants is the ability of all countries of the world to have equal access to the oil resources and to have an uninterrupted supply at a price commiserate with these countries' capacity to sustain their industrial development. But one that also preserves value for the future generations that require and need oil.

Having said that, is there any need for groups or cartels such as OPEC. Basically, are we seeing the demise of OPEC?

OPEC like any cartel was doomed to failure. There is always a net incentive for members to cheat. To produce far in excess of their quota at higher oil prices. History is rife with the remains of cartels that cave in and die because of this tendency. It's surprising that OPEC has outlived the pundits forecasts. One of the major reasons that OPEC has survived so long is the dogged consistent Saudi commitment to its survival. On closer examination one is dumbfounded by the fact that the Saudis have lost their self-interest by the protection of OPEC and OPEC quotas.

Nevertheless, 1986 represents a watershed in the sense that Saudi Arabia abandoned its strategy of supporting quotas and adopted a tit-for-tat strategy to protect its market share. Ironically, 1986 corresponds also to the year in which US imports started to rise, particularly from the Gulf region.

But even up until the Gulf War, the US imported 35 percent of its total oil requirement and imported no more than eight percent of its total requirement from the Gulf, but after the war, imports consistently started to rise. They are expected to be as high as sixty percent in a few years to come, and given the deliberate US decision to scale down domestic production, much of the extra production is coming from the Gulf region. In a way the US interest now seems to suggest that it would like to have moderate oil prices.

At work here are two conflicting interests. The US would like oil prices to remain relatively high to encourage conservation and domestic production, while at the same time it is concerned about high import bills. The historic oil prices of the late 1970s are gone forever. Then it was in the interest of the US to have high oil prices, at that time the US did not import much oil, surely not enough or anything comparable to what its competitors were importing. Today the US is a major importer of oil. The proportion of its imports are beginning to rise to what the Japanese and Germans are importing from the Gulf, and as such, would like to see oil prices very much where they are now with very limited increases in real terms.

The problem within OPEC is not much different from the problem within the G7. The G7 does not represent a monolithic homogeneous grouping. There are contradictions among the states themselves. The US interests are not similar and consistent with those of Japan and Germany. Surely the interests of Japan and Germany are for lower oil prices and greater accessibility, whereas the interest of the United States has been in the past for higher oil prices, and limited accessibility for its competitors.

In what one time, George Kenan, a major advisor to several presidents and the man responsible for the policy of containment of the former Soviet Union, had said in the 1950s- that the United States cannot afford but to exercise veto power over military industrial developments in Japan and Germany using Arab Gulf oil. What we need is some realignment and refashioning of the relationships between the consuming and the producing nations but on a more stable non-competitive and non-combative attitude, and this goes for the G7 as well as OPEC.

You have also discussed elsewhere the importance of water. You believe that water, like oil, is a strategic resource. Can you elaborate on this idea?

One is forgiven for saying that if Kuwait grew peanuts there would have been no war in the Gulf. Oil was an important factor for the very reason outlined before. But another contentious and explosive resource in the Middle East is water.

It is perhaps more important and more valuable than oil. Actually to the extent that oil is abundant in the Middle East, water is scarce relative to the demand and need, and to the explosive growth of population and industrialization. Water is becoming increasingly scarcer and scarcity brings conflict. There are three water basins in the Near East. One is the Euphrates basin. Here Syria, Iraq and Turkey share the water basin. Then the Jordan River basin, of which Syria, Lebanon, Jordan and Israel share. And then there is a whole Lebanese water basin called the Litani, although it is totally Lebanese, apparently the Israelis feel entitled to share in that water body and have moved to occupy the south part of Lebanon under a security pretext. But many feel that this is motivated by hydrological needs and imperatives.

The word rivalry, as we know it, comes from the French word *rival*, which means being on the same river and sharing riparian rights. The conflict about riparian rights seems to concentrate around entitlements to water. Iraq, for instance, feels that Turkey is acting at the expense of Iraq and Syria. This fear emanates from Turkey's Anatolian project which has about 21 damns, costing $25 billion in the north east part of Turkey and with the capacity to use 25 billion cubic metres of water. Both Iraq and Syria have been very vociferous in protecting their rights, and the situation came to blows just weeks before the invasion of Kuwait with regards to the actions of Turkey in stopping the flows of water.

Turkey seems to be moving to position itself as a water superpower in the region and using it primarily to repopulate the northeast part of Turkey with Turks instead of Kurds. It is trying to dilute the preponderant presence of cessationist Kurds. But also it is trying to project itself to the rest of the region as the only supplier of extra water and the only moderate in conflicts that are likely to arise over water.

The Jordan basin is a subject of much conflict. The issue is that Jordan does not have usable water. The Israelis have taken more than their share. What is required to irrigate is preposterous since it uses this water in a reckless way. Charging a fraction of what it costs and preventing the Palestinians and Jordanians from using it. The Israelis have sequestered over 800 million cubic metres, or over one third of available water consumption.

Now, the Lebanese situation is more crucial. Here is the Lebanese water system and Israel is calling for a share in it, charging the government with wastage. This is totally unacceptable. There are no riparian rights here at all. The Israelis have been trying to circumvent this by their occupation of South Lebanon. Water security and its dividend is increasingly vital for their survival. This water can now be used to absorb two million Russian Jews that are now coming.

The United States, Mexico and Canada are in the process of implementing a trade agreement, NAFTA. At the time of the Free Trade debates in Canada you had some dissenting comments. What is your view on NAFTA?

One needs some background. Canada is a trading country. It has always tried to reach the global market, unfortunately it depends very heavily on the American market. Ninety percent of the exports of the Province of Ontario, for example, go to the United States and also that much for imports. For Canada as a whole, upwards of 75 percent of exports go to the US and 70 percent of imports come from the US. Thus, we depend heavily on the US. Canada's health and wealth depends to a great extent on secure access to the American market.

Now, Canada has so many problems such as the recent imposition of countervailing duties, and before it, duties on wooden shingles. What we have here that most of us had expected, is a major loser in the short run. The more powerful economy will make a major take. At the time, we thought that in the long run Canada may rebound and be able to compete on a better footing. But this would require a conclusive macro-economic environment that would allow the restructuring of productive investment in a way that would make Canada more firm. The truth is that the federal government produced one of the worst and most unfriendly macro-economic environments. This included very high interest rates, an expensive dollar and the Goods and Services Tax (GST).

It is only now that the situation has become more realistic. But I am concerned that free trade is not really an issue, but fair trade is. It is impossible to have fair trade with a giant such as the United States. They have been able to extract from Canada the concessions and imposed conditions that are not maturing in any favourable way. My fear is that some of them may not be corrected, whereas the intention was that Nafta would be used to correct some of these. However, before we have a Nafta, we need to have a free trade area amongst the provinces in Canada, and we should really re-evaluate to see if free trade was really worth the costs.

Now, if Nafta is eventually ratified by the US, Canada and Mexico, I would be disappointed. My feeling is that the Mexicans might end up with as much as Canada. To Canadians, NAFTA does not mean much in terms of trade because Canada does not have much trade with Mexico- less than two percent of total trade.

Two contentious parallels remain. One is the contested market, about $70 billion of product commodities in which Mexico and Canada can compete together in the US market. They both sell the same thing- $60 billion of hard trade with the US. This might become advantageous soon, but my suspicion here is not resolved because much of the product commodity goes to the areas close to Mexico, so they really cater to the south and southwestern states. Yet Canada might be deprived of the investment that will be diverted towards Mexico. Mexico has lower labour costs, a more relaxed social programmes commitment and less stringent environmental control which might attract more investment.

Finally, as we approach the 21st century two emerging issues are the questions of globalization and international competitiveness. Is this a fair statement and what are your reflections on this?

The way disputes and contradictions are likely to be resolved, will depend to a great extent on how far the US is willing to take advantage of its military superiority, to extract and extort favourable terms for its economy vis-à-vis its competitors.

The Gulf War pointed out in a very clear and dramatic way that the Americans have the willingness and the will to do so. Perhaps, from my point of view, with a world and capital market more globalized due to freer trade than before, and with the advancement in technology, transportation and communications and the movement towards a knowledge-based capital industry; manufacturing has become mobile and able to reach areas that it didn't before. In such a world, it is very difficult and challenging for respective countries to remain competitive and to attract mobile international capital.

But the story is a little bit more severe when you take into consideration the divide between east and west, and the greater divide between north and south. We are talking about free trade, but global financial markets generate on a weekly basis 50 trillion dollars in cross-border activity. Such a massive scale, the likes of which we have never seen before; this is really about 15 times the total amount of trade that takes place in over a year.

What is very terrifying in a world with greater human mobility and greater capital mobility, is if you shun people in favour of capital, you are imposing poverty. And if people cannot move, they travel in different ways. They travel through poverty and mass exodus, the likes of which we see from Vietnam to Hong Kong and from Haiti to the United States. My feeling is that what we are seeing is the tip of the iceberg. It is going to be difficult, we are going to see more movement and mass movement. The Egyptians, if they become hungry, are most likely to march on Saudi Arabia. If the Chinese and the Indians are going to remain deprived, God help Australia. The issues are very serious. The world has become more polarized and the divide between the north and the south is now far deeper than ever before.

Dr. Atif A. Kubursi is a consultant to the United Nations and President of Econometric Research Ltd. This interview was conducted on March 1, 1993 in Toronto, Canada.

CHANGES IN THE HOUSE OF SAUD
The Beginning of the End of Petrodollars?

Jerry J. Khouri

In the West the Kingdom of Saudi Arabia has always been an enigma. This conservative Gulf state has over the past ten years undergone fundamental socio-economic and political changes, that its overall relationship with the West is seriously being questioned. Those who are questioning are not on the outside but are from within. This has raised eyebrows not only in Washington and London but also in Amman, Beirut and Cairo. Essentially, the founder of modern Saudi Arabia, King Abdul Aziz Ibn Saud, who ruled from 1932 to 1953, would find today's political and commercial culture on the streets of Riyadh, Jedda, Jubail, Yanbu and Dhahran unrecognizable.

Other than Israel, America's principal ally in the Middle East is Saudi Arabia. It not only possesses over twenty-five percent of the world's oil, but it acts as the vital link between this oil and the West. With the many disturbing domestic stories and events that have emerged over the past few years, it is the possible disruption of this link that most worries many watchers of the House of Saud.

There are two crucial issues that have permitted the rise of discontent; the profligate spending by the government and the Gulf War. With the use of oil revenues over the past fourty years, Saudi Arabia has been able to construct a nation replete with modern hospitals, highways, universities, commercial complexes, and industries. Saudis on the whole profited from all of this by enjoying free medical care and education, guaranteed employment, subsidies in the area of home purchasing, water, electricity, and telecommunications. Such social benefits from "cradle to grave" as one writer described it, spoiled the people, encouraged lethargy and built lifestyles of guarantees.

By the late 1980s and early 1990s, Saudi Arabia began to realize that such generosity can continue no more. Economic conditions became harsher as subsidies decreased, prices of daily staples increased and the nations deficit and debt were rising expeditiously. Uncertainty was prevalent not only among Saudis but also with the large expatriate community as the word unemployment suddenly became part of the economic discourse.

The Gulf War & Its Impact

When the Gulf War erupted in 1990 and 1991, the regions geopolitical concerns superseded Saudi Arabia's domestic economic worries. In order for the United States to repel Iraq's invasion of Kuwait, Saudi Arabia was used as a base to attack the Iraqi army occupying Kuwait and to bomb Iraq. When the Gulf War was "over," the bill to liberate Kuwait arrived at the desk of King Fahd Bin Abdul Aziz, the present Saudi ruler. Leading to the build up of the war, Saudi Arabia had ordered $35 billion in military hardware alone.

In the aftermath of the war, it realised that it cannot pay for the material in the manner it had agreed to, so it renegotiated payment terms. The amount was outside other costs of the war including the stationing of troops, training, damages and new commercial contracts with American companies estimated at another $35 billion. By 1993, the ramifications of the Gulf War coupled with the domestic malaise already prevalent, Saudi Arabia began to seriously deal with its increasing debt load estimated at $100 billion. In 1994, King Fahd announced a 20 percent reduction in the budget set at $42.6 billion, down from $52.5 billion the previous year. At the same time, during the 1993 to 1994 period, the kingdom's oil revenues plunged by $10 billion as oil prices decreased.

As the country tried to address its domestic financial needs, in 1994 the Saudi government strangely announced several multi-billion dollar contracts with American companies that many believed were political decisions rather than wise commercial ones. Boeing and McDonnell Douglas received a $6.0 billion order to modernize Saudia, the national commercial airline. Then came a $4.1 billion contract with AT&T to expand and modernize the national telephone service. These contracts and many others not only hurt domestic economic strategy, but upset many European nations as they believe they lost the contracts because of political pressure by the United States. By the end of 1995, as the external political fallout dissipated, Saudi Arabia began to deal with a domestic political boiling pot.

Discontent in the Land of Comfort

On November 13, 1995, the Saudi National Guard communications centre in the capital Riyadh was car bombed. When this occurred, instantly, outside agitators and agent provocateurs were accused especially from Iran. The real truth, however, was that the bombers were domestic Saudis who accuse the government of corruption and oppression. Over the past several years there has been a rise of opposition movements throughout the entire Gulf region. Many have been arrested for sedition and violence, but some are in exile. The leading Saudi opposition movement, the Committee for the Defense of Legitimate Rights (CDLR) is based in London, an irony since the United Kingdom is one of Saudi Arabia's closest friends and a strong commercial partner. In fact, the existence of the CDLR has lead many English business leaders to denounce it and have chastised the government for permitting it to operate in one of the world's leading financial cities and home for many wealthy Saudis. The reason for the anger is that the business community believes that so long as groups such as CDLR exist in London and continue to publicly denounce the Saudi royal family, British businesses will be ignored by the Saudi government.

In late June of this year, another bomb went off as this time there was an attack on a US Air Force housing complex in Dhahran in eastern Saudi Arabia. This attack coupled with the one in Riyadh has internationally exposed Saudi discontent and has propelled many to address the serious economic and social problems that persist.

The nations socio-economic realities are not encouraging. The population is 18.5 million and growing at 3.8 percent a year, with those under 20 comprising some 60 percent. The per capita GDP is a third of the $18,800 it was in 1981. With increasing poverty as attested by many welfare organizations, rising unemployment is forcing many Saudis to find "menial" jobs that were once reserved for foreign labour. Basically, as Roula Khalaf, a writer on the Middle East, explained in the *Financial Times* of London: "after decades of immense wealth and lavish spending, Saudi Arabia is adjusting to life as a normal country."

New Opportunities With a Caveat

With a new cabinet and budget in place, and a decreasing deficit, the Saudi government has begun to encourage diversification as a means of reducing dependency on oil revenues. The Saudi Export Development Centre has been created to promote and finance exports in the non-traditional sector, such as agricultural goods. In fact, with the building of ports, the creation of industrial cities such as Jubail and Yanbu, the sponsoring of advanced scientific research in areas of medicine, and projects in the areas of agriculture, dairy and animal husbandry, all are supposed to diversify exports and guarantee income outside the oil sector. There will be growth in these fields no doubt, but many economists are suspect in the belief that the non-oil sector will ever be viable enough to receive sustained income. Thus oil remains a crux of the over-all geo-economic strategy of the United States and Saudi income dependency.

Arranging Saudi Arabia's economic priorities will be a challenge. Reforms in the areas of commercial and investment law are slowly emerging. Immediate priorities revolve around government payment arrears of around $3.0 billion, while long term it is to control inflation, now hovering in the area of 4.5 percent. Another priority is to encourage the repatriation of private Arab capital estimated at an astounding $130 billion now sitting in foreign accounts such as New York, London, Geneva and Paris.

But the true challenge is political and institutional. When King Fahd fell ill in late 1995 and handed over power to Crown Prince Abdullah, his half brother, the question of political succession arose. While no rules of succession exist, two leading candidates are Abdullah and Defense Minister Prince Sultan. The challenge for Saudi Arabia is to address the political issues so as the new generation of educated Saudi youth can reap the rewards in the future. With continuing uncertainty and American meddling, Saudi discontent shows no sign of abating and this is where the concern ought to be.

COMMERCIAL POLICY ON IRAQ SPLITS WESTERN NATIONS

Jerry J. Khouri

Since the end of the Gulf war, Iraq has been subjected to a series of overlaying United Nations sponsored sanctions. Under UN Resolution 687, better known as the ceasefire resolution, Iraq's oil industry is the target. Baghdad may not sell its oil without the complete dismantlement of its chemical weapons and other weapons of mass destruction. There is a proviso for humanitarian goods, and some oil may be sold under UN supervision to help pay for some goods, but the latter has been rejected arguing it violates Iraq's sovereignty.

However, over the past year there have been visible splits within the Security Council about whether sanctions should continue. On one side there sits the United States and the United Kingdom who want to tighten the sanctions further; and on the other, France, Russia and China have advocated moderation. What is behind the division? As usual in the Middle East, commerce and oil.

Iraq is second to Saudi Arabia in the worlds proven oil reserves (see table). Before the Gulf war, Iraq was one of the Arab worlds most advanced nations in areas of industry, construction, medicine and the arts. While being advanced, its people also had to endure a brutal regime whose human rights record is well documented and is indisputable.

Proven Oil Reserves (%)

Saudi Arabia	25.89	Other	33.83
Iraq	10.01	Oman	0.47
Iran	9.29	Yemen	0.40
UAE	9.82	Qatar	0.37
Kuwait	9.41	Bahrain	0.01

Source: IMF, EIU and independents

With all that in mind, western companies hobnobbed with Baghdad for commercial and industrial interests. The invasion of Kuwait in 1990 put a halt to all this. Since then the same French, Italian, Russian and Chinese (to name some) want to return to the "glory days." Hence the debate over sanctions. Incidentally, there is another group who have been advocating the lifting of sanctions. These are the global non-governmental organizations who have

Iraqi Trade before the Gulf War

	Total Exports $12.06bn (99% oil)	Imports $10.29bn
Germany	12.5%	1.1%
US	12.3	19.2
Turkey	9.2	11.7
UK	7.9	0.7
Other EC	7.1	14.4
Japan	5.2	9.1
France	5.1	6.3
Italy	4.0	5.1
Brazil	3.7	12.7
Other	33.0	19.7

Source: Financial Times/UK Department of Trade

painstakingly audited the effects of sanctions. Their point of view is humanitarian as the children of Iraq have suffered tremendously.

Nevertheless, coupled with western interest there is Iraq's diplomatic manoeuvre. Tariq Aziz, deputy prime minister, has been talking with several countries but it was France that welcomed him personally. Aziz has met with foreign minister Alain Juppé in Paris who subsequently announced the opening of an interest section in Baghdad. This has angered the Americans and the British.

Furthermore, in late February, Iraq sponsored an international conference where several global oil company executives were in attendance. This included Elf Aquitaine, Total, Gaz de France, Agip (Italy), Repsol (Spain), Deminex (Germany), Neste (Finland), Petrobas (Brazil), Aran Energy (Ireland), Ranger Oil (Canada), Mitsubishi Oil, Samsung, Hyndia and CPC. At the conference the government announced that in post-sanctions Iraq, the oil fields will be denationalized to entice foreign capital. Most of the above companies walked away with contracts conditional upon the lifting of sanctions.

While only one British company was in attendance, that does not mean that they are indifferent. A new organization called Iraq-British Interests (IBI) was formed in London. At a meeting it was reported some 80 companies and organizations were present and some were part of the British commercial establishment. So on one hand, official government policy is to tighten resolution 687, while on the other, it is to look away on recent oil interests. And according to one reporter based in Paris, Iraq has established a global system to sell crude oil and refined products to circumvent the embargo. Some estimate that the sales have generated some U.S. $800 million over the past year.

Coincidentally, one point forgotten in all this is the role of France. While it should not be singled out, it is interesting to note that the leading candidate in the forthcoming elections, Jacques Chirac, has historically had strong ties with Iraq. Moreover, at this moment France is the president of the EU and will be the president of the Security Council in July. Such facts, amongst many, further explain the divergent attitude between Continental Europe and its ally across the Atlantic.

The debate over sanctions has not ended. This issue is very complex, as Iraq struggles to survive. Punishment of a regime is one thing, argue some seasoned observers of the region, but thus far it has been the people who have been penalized. The regime of Saddam Hussein stands tall without any imminent threat.

TIME BOMB
Dayton Peace Process Provides a Temporary Solution for the Balkans

Tihomir Mikulic

According to the statements of American experts published in the British news-paper "The Mail on Sunday", Bosnia was the most watched territory in history. The United States could see movements of troops if there were any, if some-thing was spoken, they could hear it, they could break any code in any coded material. "We have a really large quantity of material from Intelligence serv-ice," says a former employee in the Clinton Administration. "If western gov-ernments had wanted to cooperate, that would have undoubtedly led to a suc-cessful court procedure at the high level...We have everything. Everything. Actually, a few countries have communications which could proclaim the lead-ership in Belgrade guilty."

I have a feeling that these electronic gods of today, those that watch us from satellites and install political leaders to positions of power in various countries throughout the world, exactly mirror the progress of Serbian leader Slobodan Milosevic. Why is he not on trial for war crimes, while the evidence is still fresh? Why is he now covered by the cloak of peace-maker?

And what about the 200,000 to 250,000 victims in Bosnia? As much material evidence as possible of the mass murders is to be concealed. Transport bones, corpses, pour quicklime over them, dump them into mines and blast the shafts. British troops among the IFOR forces, located in Prijedor, only a mile from the place where the Serbs have been hastily destroying the evidence, do not under-take anything. Show one field of mass death; hide all of the others! Is this why the US stopped the Croatian-Bosnian offensive in north-western Bosnia in the Autumn of 1995?

The Dayton meeting was urgently convened, unseen pressures were exerted to make the victims sign a peace treaty, lines of separation were drawn and NATO itself came to the Balkans. Most of the mass torture areas and mass graves in northwestern Bosnia lie directly on the current separation line, but within the jurisdiction held and administered by Republika Srpska. Did those mass graves happen to be on the Serbian side so that the world would not find the extents of those horrors, or is it that the Serbs could hide material evidences of their atrocities undisturbed? Or both? Was that the purpose of the Dayton peace treaty, to leave the mass graves on the Serbian side of Bosnia?

The territories of northwest Bosnia around Prijedor, the area around Srebrenica and the territory of Brcko are the territories in which the largest mass graves are located. According to the data released by the United Nations centre for human rights, there are 187 mass graves in the territory of former Yugoslavia, 143 in the territory of Bosnia and Herzegovina and 44 in Croatia. What we witness now in this part of central Europe is a proliferation of new states, religions, military forces, extremisms and weapons. The Balkan barrel of gunpowder is filling up! Are western politicians carrying out a verdict against Europe itself in the process?

The Dayton Accord

The military part of the Dayton treaty negotiated between the warring parties is being carried out according to plan. IFOR took positions along the separation lines to execute the military provisions of the treaty. However, there exist problems with the execution of the civil portion of the peace treaty, which includes the building of the peace process and the nation state, with one of the most ambitious multinational peace operations ever undertaken.

The second part of the plan includes the building of a civil society, the renewal of broken international relationships, recovering of the disturbed trust between entities fighting a war against each other only yesterday, and the establishment of political institutions in Bosnia and Herzegovina. In the end, this plan is to create a stable balance between the republics of former Yugoslavia and to the establishment of a permanent peace in these territories.

For carrying out such an ambitious peace plan, the period of one year was allocated. This time frame is far too short for the realisation of such huge tasks. Even decades are needed for that. "Are we and our allies ready to take over such a program which goes far beyond the pure ensuring of peace and sets as its goal the construction of a whole state? There should be no time frame for the realisation of such a strategy."; stated former US Secretary of State Henry Kissinger, as he continued: "The only way which gives a small chance that any kind of a success be achieved is the division of Bosnia. And even that option has small chances of succeeding within the period of one year."

"Our terms are firm," wrote US Undersecretary of State Richard Holbrooke in an article published in February of this year; "IFOR will withdraw in less than a year. If we do not succeed in bringing peace to that territory within that time, it would not be good that we stay there for several years." Thus, into the Dayton treaty, the one year term limit was specified for the realisation of a strategy for which there should be no time limitation.

In addition, those responsible for this war and the horrible crimes committed, were not punished, which ought to be the first presupposition for justice for the basis of a permanent peace. Consequently, the short termism of the treaty and the lack of enforcement of an effective war crimes tribunal up to now, are two mines that have been set under the Dayton process. Moreover, the treaty is inconsistent, unrealistic and takes into account only the vain hopes in the survival of the Moslem-Croatian federation, while the essence of the Dayton peace treaty is based exactly on that Federation.

In order to carry out the civil part of the treaty, which is by far more complicated than the military aspect, former Swedish Prime Minister and special European Union envoy to the Balkans, Carl Bildt, has recently argued that it will be difficult, critical and of crucial significance for the entire peace process. Apart from any clear conceptual ideas on the execution of projects, people and money are necessary for the realization of the civil aspect of the peace treaty.

The costs of the renewal of Bosnia and Herzegovina, the costs of the operation of peace-keeping forces and for the development of everything that was anticipated in the peace treaty, require monetary commitments of some five billion dollars. From the first seven hundred million that was required for the first three months of implementing the plan, only some sixty two million dollars has been transferred, or ten percent of the overall budgeted requirement for the mission.

In short, the US Congress is not prepared to transfer large sums of money to Bosnia. Japan and the Arab countries have not shown that they are ready to pledge any substantial amounts either. Europeans are waiting and weighing their options at this moment. All eyes have turned towards Germany, but Germany remains silent. Germany has come to believe that this is not its war, and has already drawn down any surplus on the re-construction of the former east Germany after its reunification. While she continues to fight recurring recessionary elements domestically. Even the World Bank has cancelled some one hundred and fifty million dollars that it originally pledged to transfer to Bosnia.

The fact that the necessary amounts of money have not arrived for reconstruction, represents another obstacle for the successful realization of ambitious peace ideals. None of the projects in the world, even some of the best, are unable to succeed if the necessary assets for effective implementation are not secured. "It is the civil part of the agreement from Dayton that will be the trial of our success or failure, and not the military part," claims Holbrooke. "In order to register Dayton as a success, and not only as the highest point of our good intentions, the civil part must be realized successfully. So much will depend on the failure in Bosnia," Holbrooke continued; "the future of NATO, the future of the American-Russian relationship, the new role of Germany and France in a unified Europe, the national interest of the United States of America."

Since everybody is supporting the Dayton peace treaty verbally, both the Americans and Europeans, the Arabs and the Japanese, and nobody pledges the necessary assets, the chances for its success are more pessimistic than optimistic. A mine has been set under the Dayton peace process due to this very fact. Moreover, Carl Bildt, responsible for the implementation of the civil element of the treaty, complains that there is a lack of law enforcement infrastructure within the region. Consequently, it seems as though the military forces of NATO will have to succumb to the pressures of civil duties in the process. The danger being that any demonstration of force, could transform NATO into an enemy in the eyes of one or more of the parties involved.

Signs also exist of complications in the field. For one, the mass migration of Serbs from the suburbs of Sarajevo, goes in direct contrast to the civil intent of the treaty. Another point of agitation is the continued use of terrorism in isolated cases by the Bosnian Serbs. Sniper shots, rockets being targeted at trams in Sarajevo and the holding of hostages, continue to be counter-productive.

Uneasy Alliance

Violations of the civil intent of the Dayton treaty have also been made by the Muslim-Croat Federation in Bosnia. The disputes between the Croats and Muslims point to even more conflict. The heaviest blow to the Federation and the Dayton treaty was made in the town of Mostar. It started with the murder of a Croatian policeman by the Muslim side, and escalated with the Muslims breaking into two Croatian villages. Negotiations ensued with Germany as the mediator between the two sides. Animosities were further raised when German Foreign Minister Klaus Kinkel, declared that Bosnia has always been a "muslim" country, effectively siding against Germany's historical allies, the Croats.

Meanwhile, in Germany, a fierce anti-Croatian campaign was started, beginning with the cancellation of the Croatian program on radio station WDR. All of these subtle signs point to a permanent shift in political sentiments against Croatia. The initial recognition of the Croatian Republic by Germany, which meant so much to Croatia, could be missing in the future. Croatian extremism assisted in damaging Croatia's standing with the German Federal Republic.

Another problem with the Dayton peace process lies in the unclear goals originally set for IFOR. Questions over the protection of mass murder and graveside evidence uncovered surfaces on a frequent basis. IFOR is struggling to clearly define its role, as they are accused for not openly arresting those that have been charged with war crime offenses.

Analysts anticipating new complications in the Balkans have recently made their views public. The US Central Intelligence Agency (CIA) has produced through newly-appointed US Under Secretary of State Robert Galluci, and the successor to Richard Holbrooke, a warning that there exists clear possibilities for the renewal of war, after the departure of the US forces in Bosnia.

Under such a scenario, it is expected that Russia will side with the Serbs, Turkey and various Islamic countries with the Muslims, with the consequences of having new conflicts spread between the Muslim-Croat Federation. Under such a scenario, the possibility exists of a unification of the Bosnian Serbs with Serbia, and the Bosnian Croats with Croatia. With the necessity of establishing an independent Muslim state. Such a scenario brings us back full-circle to Henry Kissinger's plan, which proposed a three-way split of Bosnia into their respective ethnic regions.

It is interesting, nonetheless, that all parties are willing to swear by the Dayton peace treaty, yet the treaty itself contains many recipes for disaster. Failure, from the proposed poor conceptual solutions in the agreement, to the actual realisation in the field. The risks of having Dayton fail have very vast repercussions to the entire functioning of NATO. The future of the peace-keeping mission itself, will bring into question the future of the NATO alliance. The broader implications of any such breakdown, will harm US-Russian relations, the new role of Germany and France in Europe and the American national interest.

"The results of our efforts in Bosnia will affect that which elsewhere happens much more than we think," Holbrooke continues; "Some Americans believe that the problem of Bosnia is separated from the rest of Europe. They are wrong. Unstable Europe would threaten basic national interests of the United States of America. But, we do not know how this peace process will end."
For the moment, while IFOR maintains its positions, there will be peace between the three sides in Bosnia and Herzegovina. However, subtle infractions will continue to exist, and may lead to further escalation. Such infractions can be specifically identified as follows:

• Serbian obstruction to the basic functioning of the Dayton accord, through "petty" terrorist action
• Further strains within the Muslim-Croat alliance. The Russian newspaper *"Segodnja"* writes that the Mostar case is just the first in a long line of those awaiting Croats and Muslims, which could very easily turn into armed conflict between the two uneasy allies
• inadequate financing of the civil reconstruction of Bosnia, without which everything else will be in vain
• engagement of IFOR in civil matters, which will lead to greater conflicts
• lack of enforcement against identified war criminals
• premature withdrawal of the US forces in IFOR, possibly followed by the British and French forces. Followed by the possible replacement of troops from Islamic countries in the region

The US Central Intelligence Agency (CIA), also does not anticipate the outbreak of war between the Croats and the Serbs, while an armed conflict between the Croats and Muslim Bosnians is much more likely.

Balkan Time Bomb

It is well known that America does nothing for friendship, but for interest. Besides, the Americans have a habit to start supporting one side, and turn around in the end and support the other side. If America will support the Muslims, at the expense of the Muslim-Croat Federation, they will ultimately break this fragile association. If they break the Federation, they have effectively broken the Dayton peace accord. What is left is the original Kissinger plan, where Bosnia is a Muslim state, with part of Bosnia going to Croatia and the other part to Serbia.

An interesting remark was recently made by Bosnian government official Haris Silajdzic, regarding the possibility that the Federation, and the whole Dayton peace treaty fails. Silajdzic claims that the consequence of that failure would be the creation of an incomplete Islamic state, squeezed between a Great Serbia and a Great Croatia. He went on to say that the Bosnian army fought against such a division, but that the leadership is ready to give in.

The next step, according to Silajdzic, would be the radicalisation of the Muslim mini-state and another war within five years, in which the Croats and Serbs would endeavour to divide the remainder. In that case, he adds; "I fear we are facing larger troubles in the Balkans during the next ten years."

The initial intent of the Dayton peace process, may ironically lead to the creation of a mini fundamentalist Muslim state at the door of Europe. In that case, the Dayton treaty leaves us with many more questions, than it proposes as solutions.

THE ADRIATIC PRIZE!
US Asserts its Regional Interests

William B.Z. Vukson

Background to the War

The Kosovo crisis followed by the NATO-led military intervention in Serbia and Montenegro is a logical extension to the breakdown of the former Yugoslavia. The political instability that was created immediately after the death of Marshall Tito in 1983, culminated first in all-out war in the northern Alpine Republic of Slovenia and shortly thereafter, in Croatia. After gaining recognition as independent states through the direct sponsorship of the then

Foreign Ministers of Germany and Austria; Hans Dietrich Genscher and Alois Mock, the eventual retreat of the Yugoslav army back towards Serbia was to carry even greater consequences for what later developed in Bosnia Herzegovina and now in Kosovo.

The current state of what is left of the former Yugoslavia, uniting Serbia and Montenegro, is the only surviving country to still embrace a socialist economic system. To now, it has rejected the overall trend towards attempting to create an "emerging market" style of economic model, as it stands to symbolise a region far more significant for its religious, cultural and political institutions in todays definition of world economic and political power. The western value system of beliefs, customs and markets stops at the border between Croatia and Serbia, while the latter stands as a gateway to "eastern" traditions, a hallmark of which is a more primitive way of organising how its economy and government function.

An Economic Struggle?

Despite these differing cultural and religious characteristics of the former members of Yugoslavia, the cold economic interpretation of the current and past conflicts in the region have to do with the former power structure of the country and the way in which Marshall Tito managed to hold the region together in a defined unitary state. During the glory days of Yugoslavia, the Republic of Serbia with its larger population base was the centre of political power. Belgrade was the capital and the core diplomatic seat, with a massive amount of funds being repatriated to the region of Serbia from economic activity in other parts of the country.

The Adriatic Coast attracted large numbers of tourists from Germany, Italy and the UK, making it the most vital foreign exchange generator in the country. Most of the money that was made from tourism in a region that was part of Croatia, ended up in Belgrade and mainly went into the military-industrial apparatus of the former Yugoslavia, at the great expense of developing infrastructure in other parts of the country. The Adriatic Coast was the most vital economic foundation for the former Yugoslavia, and has slowly evolved into being a vital region to US interests over the past decade. All of the wars that broke out in what were the former Republics making up Yugoslavia were partially, if not fully motivated by the desire to control the revenues coming from tourism from the unspoiled beauty of this region of the Mediterranean Coast.

Growing US Interests

After the recognition of independence for both Slovenia and Croatia came first from Germany and Austria, closely followed by that of the European Community for the two break-away Republics, the US overtook the initiative after the election of the Clinton Administration, by re-arming the Croatian military and giving advice for its own protection and eventual expulsion of the militant Krajina Serbs. The US moved to expand its interests in the Balkans after the civil war broke out in Bosnia, and was the ultimate sponsor and broker of the Dayton Peace Accords that continue to bind the country together to this day.

The US is not only the pivotal power in NATO, but is also the leading advocate and financier of the IMF and the World Bank. The latter two institutions being very active in refinancing the fledgling market economies in central and eastern Europe. Both financial and military power are currently working for US and western interests in the region, where countries such as Bulgaria, Romania, the Ukraine and Macedonia, are directly dependent on IMF loans to avert potential defaults on money borrowed from private banks and the Eurobond markets. Even the Serbian traditional ally, Russia, is finding it very difficult to cope with the default in the summer of 1998, that continues to plague its economy and its access to private international capital markets. On-going discussions with the IMF and the World Bank, have handcuffed an effective Russian response to the needs of Serbia.

Plan for Reconstruction

After the bombing ends, a massive bill to the tune of $60 billion will await the world community. The lasting effects of the bombing have already destroyed the tourist season in Croatia, Slovenia and Bulgaria, with very grave repercussions for their trade balance accounts. The fledgling stock and capital markets in Bucharest, Budapest, Sofia, Zagreb and Ljubljana, operate under a continuous threat of bankruptcy, as trading volumes in even the best companies collapse, with foreign interest nowhere in sight. Add to this scenario a very unstable banking system and massive illiquidity, and the IMF and World Bank see an increasingly ominous role to play in the region to revive the fledgling market system. Already, a number of central bank Governors and political officials in these countries have requested a massive US-led bail-out of debts that are paralysing the region, while the promise of development or venture capital financing has been bogged-down at the institutional as well as local levels of incompetence.

The real difficulties in establishing a lasting stability, security and peace in the entire region of central and eastern Europe will merely escalate after the bombing ends. With growing political and economic distress visible in Russia by the day, any long term solution through a market based system can only be achieved through a massive financial commitment by the United States in the entire region. To begin, an effective commitment for reconstruction and for market stability should come in the form of a substantial transfer of a large portion of the current US budget surplus.

NORTH AMERICAN POLITICAL SCENE

These are both a U.S. and Canadian-oriented series of articles that address certain specific issues in the 1990s. In "Reflections on the Changing Face of Canadian Foreign Policy" the author goes into the new framework on "trade policy" initiatives that the Canadian government started promoting in the 1990s. In contrast to more traditional pillars of foreign policy, including peacekeeping initiatives, human rights and playing the role of global intermediary, the new Canadian framework encouraged an aggressive promotion of Canadian business in winning foreign contracts and procurement regardless of these countries' human rights and environmental history.

The interview "The 1996 Presidential Primaries Through the Corner of an Eye," were conducted just prior to the election and the ensuing eruption of the Monica Lewinsky scandal. On the surface, the U.S. economy was performing well, only to get better as the decade came to a close. However, can the same be said if a "quality of life" standard was ever the benchmark instead of raw economic data? Moreover, the media went wild over Monica, just as they had done with the O.J. Simpson trial a few years back. It seems that the absence of a well-defined "enemy" and the convenient "black and white" scenario readily provided by the Cold War have been sadly missed by U.S. formulators of opinion.

Both "What Does 'Monica' Mean?" and "Beltway Coup!" by Paul Nielsen, delve deep into U.S. party politics, and try to identify the differences between Democrats and Republicans in this new era. How has the post Cold War period defined the U.S. political party system, and are there any true detectable differences between the parties of the mainstream when it comes to straight policy endorsements?

W.b.z.V.

REFLECTIONS ON THE CHANGING FACE OF CANADIAN FOREIGN POLICY
A Bolder More Assertive Period May Be Emerging

Jerry J. Khouri

In early 1995, law makers produced a review of Canadian foreign policy. This
was the third such endeavour in the past twenty-five years. The first was in
1970 under the leadership of Pierre Trudeau, in an era where Cold War dema-
goguery was thriving. The second, in the mid-1980's under Brian Mulroney, a
time where international competitiveness, internationalism and security pre-
dominated. Now in 1995, a very different global architecture exists, where
terms like post-cold war and new world order are liberally interjected. Canada
is now operating under a different light: an order where borders are porous,
where sovereignty is challenged, and where capital markets, exports and trade
dominate the tables of global forums.

During the past couple of years, the Canadian government has changed the
image of foreign policy, while simultaneously delineating substantive changes.
The Chrétien government has undertaken a "Team Canada" approach, whereby
government officials with business leaders travel to various regions to identify
and construct a new relationship with new markets. The focus thus far has been
with the developing areas like the dynamic Asian region and the up and coming South American nations. Team Canada was not there to discuss political
matters such as human rights, development and aid; rather they were there to
construct commercial contracts and to instill trade regimes.

This nuance is very important. As the foreign policy review report notes, "the
foreign economic policies of Canadian governments can determine largely how
Canada interacts with that environment." In other words, so long as trade relations are secure, the rest is secondary. This has obviously brought mixed
reviews from Canadians. The business community applauds the government's
aggressive marketing of Canada and its services. They maintain that by
increasing trade and exports, Canadians may have a better leverage if political
disputes arise. This philosophy emanates partly from Canada's traditional success as a trading nation. Also, its philosophical base is grounded in purely commercial and economic terms.

Conversely, non-governmental organizations and human rights workers argue
that this policy shift is a betrayal of Canadian history and tradition. This
Liberal government, they argue, has transformed foreign policy into a trade
policy thus ignoring the domestic environment of countries such as China,
Burma, and Indonesia. The irony of this, of course, is that during the govern-

ment of Brian Mulroney, arguably Canada's most conservative and pro-business Prime Minister, trade was linked to human rights. Mulroney's unflagging opposition to the pernicious apartheid regime, and his unwillingness to trade with South Africa was a global success story. Today all this has changed.

But several questions need to be asked. Can Canadians in this "new environment" balance trade with human rights work? Does Canada have the international power and prestige to set an example? Can the two camps in this debate come together, or are they so ideologically determined that a consensus is fruitless? These questions underscore the painful dilemmas that beset this changing nation. One of the reasons Canada has shifted its policy is not only because of foreign markets and globalization, but also domestic Canada, economically, culturally and politically, at this time is in neutral.

The inability of domestic Canada to find a niche in the 90's is troubling. The overlapping territories of social policy, economic growth, unemployment and political pluralism seem to function at cross purposes, thus stalling any vibrancy. It is here where domestic failure becomes foreign policy, thus promoting trade at any price.

Undoubtedly, pin-pointing the reasons why Canadian foreign policy has shifted is difficult. But surely, one of the reasons must be that we find foreign markets more attractive than domestic ones. North America as a whole is experiencing a cultural re-definition, that while domestic anguish persists, far away territories relieve tension. While America becomes truculent and isolationist, Canada is looking outwards. Chrétien's denouement seems to be trade! trade! trade!, not jobs! jobs! jobs!

THE 1996 PRESIDENTIAL PRIMARIES THROUGH THE CORNER OF AN EYE

International Voice Among Emerging US Isolationism

Interview with: **Michele Fratianni,**

Advisor to; President's Council of Economic Advisers (1981-82); European Commission; Italian Minister of Industry; Italian Minister of the Treasury; Tecnovalori Mutual Fund (Milan); Banca Nazionale dell'Agricoltura (Rome); Istituto Bancario San Paolo di Torino (Turin); Confindustria (Rome); Banque Bruxelles Lambert (Brussels); Argus Research Corporation; Fondigest (Milan). Currently Bundesbank Professor of International Monetary Economics, Free University of Berlin & AMOCO Professor of Business Economics & Public Policy, Indiana University

Directed by: **William B.Z. Vukson**

Domestic Issues

Why are there no credible left-wing alternatives in the US any longer?

I have three points. First, the demand for left-wing ideas and programs has been traditionally filled by a sizable part of the Democratic party, which has pushed successfully for an expansion of the welfare state. While the level of the welfare state is smaller in the US than in most industrial countries, the growth rate is not. What is absent in the US, is the strident left-wing rhetoric

---

Canadian Exports By Region (1993)

Total: $187.3 billion Cdn.

United States	80%
Western Europe	7
Japan	5
Asia/Pacific	4
Latin America/Caribbean	2
Other	2

Source: Statistics Canada

which instead prevails in France, Italy, or the United kingdom.

This reflects in part the democratic "heritage" of the US and the virtual absence of class divisions. Second, the cost of setting up a new party is not trivial. The few attempts have met with failure because the established parties have adjusted to new claims and to the changed mood of the electorate. Finally, left-wing ideas are considered extremist in the US, whose electorate has been, on the whole, pragmatic. To that, one must add that the climate for left-wing ideas is today at a historic low point.

What has been the basis behind the US electorate to move even more to the right?

The US electorate is not ideological. Past experiences have taught many voters that government does not have the solution to many of the economic and social problems of the day. Furthermore, voters have understood that many government programs benefit narrow interest groups, the bureaucracy that supervises such programs, and the consultants that advise government agencies. Finally, the US electorate has not been the only one in retrenching from leftist solutions. Certainly, the US has provided inspirations to other countries to adopt market solutions. One of the good fortunes of the US is that there is a healthy skepticism about government.

What will be the main economic/business themes in the 1996 presidential campaign?

I see two themes: the budget and the trade deficit. The US has been agonizing about fiscal deficits since the mid 1980s, that is after the first Reagan presidency. We have gone through several tax increases, including one that critically damaged former President George Bush, and the deficit remains. Tax increases lower the deficit in the short run, but have modest effects in the long run. The Republican Congress, which had an opportunity to alter radically the growth of transfer payments, is now following the standard, time-honored, strategy of reducing the tax burden first and cutting expenditures in the future. Such a strategy is flawed by the inability of the current Congress to tie the hands of future legislators, that is, it is time-inconsistent. We do not know the final outcome of the fiscal package, but the odds favor that the fiscal crisis will continue. To resolve it, legislators have to gain control over the growth of government spending.

The second economic issue involves the trade deficit. Since 1985 the US government, both in isolation and in cooperation with the other members of the G7 group, have pursued a policy of dollar depreciation with the aim of correcting its external imbalance. Furthermore, the US government has progressively engaged in an active trade policy, particularly with respect to Japan. The motivation underlying this policy is the belief that the US has a trade deficit because other countries, but especially Japan, do not play "fairly." This is a misguided concept. Our trade deficit has little to do with unfair trade practices and a great deal with the fact that the US saves too little relative to its investment needs.

Trade deficits will persist so long as the saving-investment imbalance remains. Further devaluations of the dollar and a more aggressive trade policy are a minor force in rectifying our trade deficit. Yet, much of the public looks at international trade as a horse race. A trade imbalance is understood to be a sign of lower US competitiveness and not as the result of an imbalance of saving and investment. The politicians are doing their best to reinforce these incorrect views.

What is lacking in the US economy at this very moment?

The US has been on an expansion path since the end of 1991. From a cyclical point of view, the economy is doing well.

Has the economy been largely driven by pent-up demand over the past two years?

Given that consumption accounts for almost two-thirds of total income, it is virtually impossible that real growth can occur without growth in aggregate consumption. In fact, real consumer spending last year rose 3.2 percent, approximately in line with the growth in real incomes.

Is there a creative alternative to the stale Democratic/Republican political and economic debate?

I have addressed the issue above. Let me add that there is a fair chance that Ross Perot's party can spoil the feast to both Democrats and Republicans, in the sense that the two traditional parties may have to make concessions.

Why has the standard of living become progressively worse in the US for average workers?

Between 1973 and 1994, real compensation per employed person in the US has been the lowest among the G-7 grouping. More importantly, income growth was flat in the mid range of the income distribution and sharply negative at the bottom. The situation is somewhat better if one considers family incomes as opposed to individual wage income. Information and technological advances are an important reason underlying these phenomena. The gap between workers with a great deal of human capital and specific skills and workers with low human capital and no specific skills, has risen and seems to be bound to widen further.

Furthermore, today's more competitive environment is forcing old or formerly protected industries to adjust (e.g. banking). Consequently, job tenure has diminished, which in turn has raised the anxiety level. Twenty years ago, jobs were more secure because markets were less competitive. The US automobile industry is a good example: auto wages were almost twice as high as the average manufacturing wages. The globalization of markets was bound to reduce and eliminate the rents from protection. Banking, which is being deregulated, is another sector which will undergo deep adjustments. What goes in the US will most likely spread to other industrial countries. The reason workers feel more secure in Europe has to do with regulation which keeps unemployment rates high.

World Institutions

What are your views on the curtailment in expenditures on global institutions such as the IMF, World Bank and the United Nations by the US Congress?

It is part of the larger cyclical retrenchment from world affairs. This movement is grounded in the public who has little interest in world affairs. It is not a new phenomenon. The US, by economic and political power, is expected to exert leadership in the democratic world; yet US presidents have a hard time in convincing a lethargic public. There is a resurgence of interest in world affairs in times of crises only.

The International Monetary Fund (IMF) and the World Bank are not household words; they are known to specialists. Both are post World War II institutions, which aimed at addressing problems that have been superseded or are not believed to be as critical. The IMF was the "arbiter" of the gold-dollar exchange standard; the World Bank was to foster economic development and rectify a variety of market failures. The gold-exchange standard is long gone; yet, the IMF is very much alive and has moved into new business areas, such as debt rescheduling and lending to developing countries. Our understanding of market failures has been tempered by experience, namely we recognize that for every market failure there is a government failure.

One must clearly differentiate between aid and loans for development. Aid is given for humanitarian or political reasons (that is to enhance the giving country's interests). A country, especially an important country like the US, tends to view foreign aid as part of its foreign policy. A multilateral aid agency, like the World Bank, severs this link; hence, the opposition. Furthermore, some of the World Bank lending could have been handled by private financial institutions. In such cases, the loan recipients prefer to borrow from the World Bank, because they receive a subsidy. It is hard to justify economically such a subsidy.

The United Nations is a much more visible institution than the two Bretton Woods institutions above, but it is considered ineffective. People have a perception that the UN is a "talk forum" for government officials that supports an elite of very well-paid bureaucrats. Calls for international cooperation become effective, only when a handful of critical countries decide that it is in their interest to take action. The UN is the best on-going example of the high costs of organizing and sustaining international cooperation. Having said that, there is no excuse for the US to be in arrears in its UN contributions.

How can these institutions be reformed to be more accountable or better performing?

To begin with, we need to spell out clearly their objectives and the means to meet them. For example, people are confused about the objectives of the IMF and the World Bank. These two institutions are increasingly competing for the same activities. Secondly, national governments ought to spell out why membership in such organizations is important for the national interest. Calls for world brotherhood are too generic to persuade an inward-looking electorate.

Finally, the working of these institutions should be made more transparent. To the "average voter" the IMF is mysterious. The mystery is grounded in reality, because member governments are most unwilling to let the Fund tell to the world what it does. For example, the staff of the Fund produce a lot of useful country reports which could be used by the private sector to assess and monitor country risk. These reports, however, are not available to the public.

In your view, what has been the big economic/financial disappointment in the US?

The political inability to understand the source of the US trade imbalance, and the shift towards strategic trade policy. While I agree with some of the implications of the newer international trade literature, I find that it has been used to justify the traditional positions and prejudices, and against free trade.

Regional Centres of Influence

What can you tell us is the big difference between the US-Japan relationship as opposed to the emerging US-German relationship?

The large bilateral imbalance between the US and Japan is contributing to the deterioration in the relationship between these two countries. It is ironic that as the US was developing an inferiority complex vis-à-vis Japan, this country was undergoing a deep economic crisis. In the 1960s, Japan grew at an average annual rate of ten percent, in the 1970s at 4.7 percent, and in the 1980s, all the way up to 1991 at 4.1 percent. However, since 1992, growth has fallen below one percent. The factors at work are the deflation of the real estate price bubble; the deterioration of the quality of bank assets that threaten a financial crisis; the sharper slowdown of Japanese exports following an appreciating yen, and pressures on Japan to reduce its current account surplus.

The restructuring process from an export-oriented to a domestic-oriented economy is slower than anticipated, and is responsible for part of the economic slowdown. But, another reason why Japan is underperforming, has to do with a lethargic economic policy that has failed to recognize the importance of a healthy financial system for the economy as a whole. The US government is obsessed with its trade bilateral imbalance, and has not had a full appreciation of the difficulties Japan finds itself in. There should be no rejoicing in a slow growing Japan. A resumption of the three to four percent growth of which Japan is capable is in the interest of the US and the world at large.

Germany has become relatively more important for the US because of the pivotal role played in the European Union. However, I am not inclined to exaggerate the switch in preferences. The Southeast Asian countries are growing more rapidly than the rest of the world, and sooner or later, Japan will exert a critical role in the integration process of these economies. Thus, Japan will remain very important for the US.

In a comparative sense, what is the biggest difference among the US, Japanese and German economies?

The US tends to be more market oriented. Economic policy is based on the transparency of market transactions, and on the principle that players should have equal power and equal access to information. In both Germany and Japan, the transparency issue is less important. Differences in information sets are tolerated and so is concentration of economic power. Banks and financial institutions play a more active role in the restructuring of corporations. Germany is the prototype of universal banking. The US is the prototype of the division between commercial and investment banking, although this division is now breaking down.

The other big difference has to do with labor markets. In the US labor markets are much more competitive than in Japan and Germany. Union representation is small in the US and high in Germany. Labor contracts are decentralized in the US and centralized in Germany. Labor flexibility is high in the US and low in Germany. Job tenure is low in the US and high in Germany and Japan. The Boards of German corporations have labor representatives, whereas labor does not participate in US management decisions. Japan is closer to the German model than to the US model, although the traditional "parental" role of Japanese corporations is beginning to break down.

Financial Credibility

Has the Federal Reserve maintained a credible monetary policy over the past year?

I believe so. Greenspan has been a good Chairman, like Paul Volcker before him. I hope he will be re-appointed.

How can you account for the continuous underperformance in the US dollar?

There is no shortage of theories. One theory has it that the exchange rate will move to equilibrate the current account balance. Since the US has a large current account deficit, the dollar depreciates so as to induce US residents to buy less foreign produced, and more domestically produced goods and services. This process has been going for some time. The interesting question is whether the exchange rate alone can redress the US trade imbalance? I am skeptical on this point.

What must the G-7 agenda for coordinating policies adopt towards the new century?

I am not a great believer in grand designs of coordination. Some governments wish a return of the Bretton Woods system. There is an experiment of this sort currently in the European Union, called the European Monetary System. Such a system has worked with mixed success. The events of September 1992 and August 1993, have shown the fragility of the fixed exchange rate system in the face of asymmetric shocks (e.g. German monetary union). Coordination is feasible when preferences are compatible. It follows that the first step for a grand design of coordination must start with an examination of how compatible national preferences correspond with respect to a variety of issues, including exchange rate agreements.

WHAT DOES "MONICA" MEAN?
US Media Go Wild!

Paul Nielsen

As the rest of the world watches in astonishment at the goings-on in Washington over the Monica Lewinsky affair, it is fruitful to examine the causes of this mean-spirited attempt to sully the reputation of a president using his alleged romance with a nubile young woman. Because the quest for Bill Clinton's political hide is unrelated to suborning perjury, obstruction of justice or the immature femme fatale engulfed at the centre of this maelstrom. Its life is as a result of deeply held concerns about this president personally and his place in history; doubts that are now shared by many positioned at varying points across the broad American political spectrum.

To be sure, a certain amount of the resentment comes from the political "Right," or conservative movement. They have not forgiven the American voters for rejecting George Bush and Bob Dole in successive presidential elections; thereby granting this "rube from Arkansas" the chance to become only the twelfth man in history to occupy the world's most important office for eight years. But it is incorrect to assert, as Hillary Clinton has done, that the president's troubles are solely the result of a right-wing conspiracy to destroy him. The "conspiracy" is more broadly based; and has its roots in something other than political ideology. Governor Christine Todd-Whitman of New Jersey correctly observed that the Right is not sufficiently co-ordinated and does not possess enough influence with the American public to sustain this enmity on its own. The assistance it has received should fascinate those enamoured of and interested in US politics. For it reveals more uncomplimentary details about the nature of Washington than any revelations about sexual peccadilloes could.

The US capital is consumed by a parochial prejudice that is often misunderstood by outsiders. Its simplicity does not conceal its provincial underpinnings. Succinctly put: "no one should be president without first 'paying his dues' in Washington." Jimmy Carter had difficulties with a Congress controlled by his own Democrats largely because of their resentment of his successful presidential campaign as a "Washington outsider." Even Ronald Reagan faced some well-concealed hostility from moderates within his own party for similar reasons. While they were happy to ride his coat-tails to their own individual successes, behind his back their "Beltway bias" foiled his attempts to confront the Democratic congressional leaders and their domestic policies. To a much larger degree, Bill Clinton has suffered this same fate. His first budget was almost rejected by the Democratic Congress. The 1993 health care proposal was a dismal failure, largely because moderate Democrats did not use their influence with the president to seize the initiative and close a deal when many Republicans, including Bob Dole, conceded that universality was "doable." Their political inertia and the First Lady's stridently leftist agenda ruined any possible reform. That Clinton was a former governor, from a small impoverished southern state without previous national experience, had as much to do with the results of those initiatives as did their content.

The press, particularly the print media, now has a stake in this tawdry episode. Maligned for years by the Right as a lackey for the country's liberal constituency, the mainstream press has justifiably struggled with the personal life of Bill Clinton. Is it important to the country for the president to be sexually faithful to his wife when, to all appearances, that wife appears comfortable with her position as the spouse of an unrepentant philanderer? This question has not been answered; but the media's voracious appetite for this story reflects its anger at the man for his recklessness. Clinton was given a pass when Gennifer Flowers decided to use his 1992 presidential campaign to profit from whatever notoriety one acquires by disclosing her own sexual misguidedness. The reporting about the Paula Jones case has, by any reasonable assessment, been as restrained as possible given the salacious details alleged and its historical significance as the first civil lawsuit that any Chief Executive has had to defend while in office. But despite this even-handedness and the necessity of his giving evidence under oath for an impending trial, Clinton apparently behaved, not as Caesar's wife, but as a modern day Caligula, using his position to dally with the ladies. Consequently, Kathleen Willey is only one of many women of dubious credibility who now have the attention of the nation as they recount their alleged amorous experiences with the president.

If this careless conduct has repulsed some in the press, it has made conservatives purple with rage at the apparent double standard working on the president's behalf. Bob Packwood could not remain in the Senate after he was unmasked as a sexual predator of the women in his office. Despite a distinguished career in the Senate and the appointment by one of the most popular presidents of this century, John Tower was not confirmed as Secretary of Defense, primarily because of his libidinous escapades with female subordinates. When the facts were revealed about these two Republicans, they were branded as dirty old men and sexual culprits, unsuitable for high political office. However, those same allegations, in and of themselves, do not yet disqualify Bill Clinton from the highest political office. The general public and the women's groups, who so vigilantly drove Packwood and Tower to political disgrace, now seem unconcerned about the president's similar conduct. This has the Rush Limbaughs and Jerry Falwells of America literally beside themselves.

But perhaps the most cogent explanation for the incredible "legs" of this story involves the historical assessment of this administration. Bill Clinton is presiding over the most buoyant set of political circumstances that any US president has enjoyed in at least 70 years. Not since Theodore Roosevelt was president have the economic, political and foreign relations factors operated so positively in US favour. The world is remarkably free of war; and with the exception of a few isolated rogue states of the likes of Iran and Libya, the prospect of enduring military totalitarianism seems remote.

BELTWAY COUP!
Will the New Millennium Belong to Congress?

Paul Nielsen

Now that the House of Representatives has passed two articles of impeachment against President Bill Clinton, the speculation about his ultimate fate is consuming Washington. Since the necessary twelve Democrats will probably not defect and vote with the Republicans in an upcoming Senate trial, conviction and removal from office is unlikely. With the elections in 2000 promising to be the most critical in years, anointing Al Gore now with the presidency and the advantages of an incumbent would be counter-productive. So why not just censure the man and get on with life? Perhaps the answer lies not in the individuals involved but in historical precedent. This exercise in constitutional gamesmanship should not now be seen as an effort to embarrass this president or sully his reputation. Impeachment for obstruction of justice and perjury together with Clinton's numerous humiliating apologies for his conduct have already accomplished that. Bill Clinton is now the victim of conservative scheming to preserve their social agenda and reverse a trend in presidential politics that began almost 100 years ago. "Monica" and the end of the Cold War have provided Congress with a unique opportunity to regain constitutional dominance; and that more than anything else explains their current intentions.

Watergate or McCarthyism?

Commentators have written about this episode *ad nauseum* drawing inaccurate parallels to Watergate. Some have astutely compared the Independent Counsel's investigation to those carried out by Senator Joseph McCarthy in the 1950s. Can anyone doubt that the sudden resignation of Bob Livingston as Speaker-elect does not signal that "sexual blacklisting" is now afoot in Washington? But this tawdry spectacle cannot be dismissed as mere witch-hunting by Ken Starr and other conservatives. It has its roots in the intentions of the Founding Fathers for the presidency, the constant struggle between the executive and legislative branches of the government for constitutional supremacy and conservative fears that their professed moral agenda has lost its hold on the American electorate.

Presidential Power

It is now virtually impossible to regard any president as the mere ceremonial Head of State and check on Congressional excess that was his original mandate. His pre-eminence as the "most powerful man on Earth" predates us. However, the Framers of the Constitution, fearful of the "tyranny of the King," clothed the presidency with less constitutional power than that granted to the

Prime Minister in a parliamentary democracy. While Parliament in England was originally intended as a check against the Crown, the presidency was never meant to be more than a counter-balance to the inexorable will of the people as expressed by their elected and (in the case of the Senate until 1913) appointed representatives in Congress. Consequently, a president is powerless to legislate; and cannot successfully prevent any statute from becoming law in the face of a two-thirds majority in both houses of Congress.

Until the 20th century, presidents acquired the authority we have now come to accept as an integral part of the office only by the force of their personalities and stature (Washington, Jackson); the magnitude of their accomplishments (Jefferson with the Louisiana Purchase and the Declaration of Independence) or the imperilling of the nation (Madison with the War of 1812 and Lincoln on the Civil War). So long as the United States was a new country, wrestling with its own identity and settling its vast territories, this ceremonial presidency sufficed. But the decline of the European powers, evidenced by their willful death march toward the self-immolation of the Great War, created a diplomatic vacuum which the USA was uniquely positioned to fill. It was Theodore Roosevelt who first recognised America's new place in the world; and using his "bully pulpit," he created the first "imperial presidency" to fulfill that role, putting Congress on the defensive ever since. His progressiveness was an intriguing contradiction to Europe's failure to eradicate the unworkable distinctions of class that doomed their societies. Could the United States have built and retained the Panama Canal if anyone less dynamic than Teddy Roosevelt had been president and Europe had not been so absorbed in its own anachronistic alliances?

In the last 90 years the presidency has been populated by great men who rose to the occasion, using Roosevelt's example to carve out their own personal majesty. Woodrow Wilson's triumphant tour of Europe after World War I and the League of Nations was an acknowledgment by the world of the American president's influence. The Senate's ultimate rejection of the League was Congress's feeble attempt to win back the constitutional initiative. It was too little, too late; for it was then impossible to relegate any president against his will to mere ribbon cutting and baby kissing, (although some like Taft, Coolidge and Eisenhower appeared to yearn for nothing more). The president's power rested upon his use of moral authority to by-pass Congress and appeal directly to the American people. FDR's New Deal and Lend-lease, Truman's Marshall Plan and the Truman Doctrine, the civil rights legislation of JFK and LBJ, and Reagan's tax cuts and thinning of the federal bureaucracy are examples.

Since 1900 Congress has dominated only those presidents who abdicated the power bequeathed by TR (Taft, Coolidge), presided over corrupt administrations (Harding, Nixon), demonstrated a compelling ineffectiveness as leaders (Hoover, Carter) or lacked any coherent vision of the future to define their initiatives (Bush). Conservatives are now attempting to consign Bill Clinton to this ignominy; and ironically, it is his devastating lack of moral authority with the American people, not conviction in the Senate, that is their most effective weapon. While he may remain in office, his numerous prevarications will prevent the public from signing on to anything involving dramatic sacrifice such as saving Social Security or significant health care reform.

Republican Search for Identity

Bill Clinton is despised by conservatives because he personifies their worst fears that the "family values" platform so successful for them in national elections is not a pervasive moral imperative for Americans, but rather a rallying point for the narrow, white "Bible Belt" constituency that has hijacked the GOP. This may explain the incomprehensible "job satisfaction" ratings in the high 60's for Clinton despite the prevailing belief that he is a liar and personally untrustworthy. Republicans fear that his ability to remain effective in office will be accepted as proof that their cultural war against the "free love" and unrestrained self-indulgence of the 1960s has been lost. (The number of conservative Republicans guilty of flagrant marital infidelities is perhaps further proof). Speaker-elect Bob Livingston had to resign, not for his adultery, but because to support him would constitute rejection of the Puritanism that has always been an article of faith with Republican core constituencies. If we have to accept adultery as a fact of 21st century life, can abortion be far behind? Not even the Democrats have enough courage to verbally confirm this reality; so the Senate must conduct this "show trial" knowing that a conviction is not possible or even desirable, mindful that the precise details of the tryst (which must be aired to establish Clinton's perjury) will forever identify them as sexual McCarthyites. The facts will not so much elucidate Clinton's mendacity as it will their own sanctimony.

Johnsonising Clinton

The deal for censure will be struck when Republicans are convinced that they have finally "Andrew Johnsonised" Bill Clinton. For this impeachment of the president is identical to the only other in America's history. Johnson was Lincoln's successor, a southern Democrat chosen by the Great Emancipator to heal the wounds caused by the Civil War. The counts of impeachment alleged that his dismissing Edwin Stanton as Secretary of War violated an ambiguous law regarding presidential authority to replace Cabinet members. But the real motivation was his opposition to the punitive Reconstruction sought to be imposed upon the South by a Congress dominated by northern Republicans. That they failed to convict (by one vote) was unimportant. Johnson's effectiveness as an opponent to their calculated oppression had ended. He faded into obscurity; rejected by his own party as their presidential candidate for 1868. Then as now legislators were belittling a troublesome president whose authority was antagonistic to their plans. Too much of the Republican agenda which has for so long been the holy grail of the conservative movement in the United States is jeopardised by "l'affaire Monica." It will not do for someone with Bill Clinton's intellectual capabilities and the moral authority he lacks to restate the principles underpinning American politics. To paraphrase Marc Antony, they have come to bury Clinton not to destroy him!

ITALY AS THE CROSSROADS OF THE COLD WAR AND AFTER

The assassination of the President of the Christian Democrats, Aldo Moro, in the 1970s by the Red Brigades plunged Italy into crisis and signalled the spread of Communism, to the dismay of the U.S. and western European countries. These were the peak of the Cold War years, and the succession of Italy into the G7 was as much a political and strategic move to ensure that it remained an integral part of free market ideology, as much as it was a move that honoured its economy as being the third largest in Europe; even ahead of the U.K.

As the old system collapsed in 1989, so went the political protectors of U.S. and free market interests. The 1990s were significant since Italy joined the single European currency, and more than at any time in history had to implement free market elements to its program, much to the dismay of the special interest groups that have come to define the boundaries of business, labour and the civil service. The election of the Freedom Alliance in 1994, with former media tycoon Silvio Berlusconi as Prime Minister, even though he still had to answer to a countless array of corruption charges in handling his business affairs during the Cold War years, was an outcome that signalled an end to the old political power structure with the disintegration of many of the old traditional parties, including the Christian Democrats.

In our short interview with Berlusconi, it was clear that he admires the free market ideologies of Margaret Thatcher and Ronald Reagan, including a more decentralised governmental structure; gaining the support of the separatist "Liga Nord," which has called for the outright secession of the northern Italian states from the south. Further, Berlusconi has come out against

Italy's participation in the single European currency project right from the start. Even though his government was short-lived, he remains a permanent political fixture in Italy with the prospect of regaining power, and leading Italy to further deregulation and free marketisation.

W.b.z.V.

FIRST LEADER OF THE SECOND ITALIAN REPUBLIC

Interview with: **Silvio Berlusconi**

Directed by: **Antonio Nicaso**

Prior to becoming Prime Minister elect, Silvio Berlusconi held a controlling interest in Italian holding company, Fininvest. Fininvest consists of: Television (3 national channels: Italia Uno, Rete Quattro, Canale Cinque), Publishing (il Giornale, Mondadori), Retailing (Standa Department Stores), Sports (AC Milan). Who could have imagined that the new Italian Prime Minister would have been someone entirely new to the political scene. Media tycoon Silvio Berlusconi, within three months, has managed to put together a party entirely from scratch, and has guided it to victory in the recent March parliamentary elections. In a brief interview granted to The G•7 Report, the new Prime Minister reflects on his political candidacy and outlines his coalition government's immediate agenda.

Why did you decide to enter politics?

The love for my country. It occurred to me last summer when Parliament passed the new electoral law that I had no choice but to enter into politics. With this new law, we were running the risk of losing Italy to the leftists, who pretend to be liberals, but deep down are for greater government control and statism.

The centre was shattered, and the rightists were tattered. I tried to convince them to come to an agreement and form a coalition team, but my efforts were in vain. Consequently, in three months, I have created a political party from scratch by putting together 400 candidates. I have organized the election campaign and have said to myself: my life as a business man; as an industrialist, is over! This phase of my existence is closed and the political one is about to begin. I am even prepared to sell my corporations, if I could find buyers in this harsh market. Provided that the loyalty and hard work of those that have followed me would be honoured and compensated.

To reiterate, you would sell everything; truly sell?

I am prepared to go even beyond the U.S. norm (blind trust). My life as an entrepreneur is coming to an end. I am in politics now and have surpassed the initial difficulties. However, there is still a lot of work to do. Of this, I would like to convince even those that used to think I was crazy.

How are you going to manage the divergent interests within your coalition between Fini's neo-fascist National Alliance and Bossi's separatist Lombard League? How do you view the acts of Fini's young supporters; the greetings (with the right hand slanted upwards) just after the election victory of your government?

I know, especially abroad, that certain gestures and the praises of Fini to Mussolini have made a bad initial impression, and I realize that there is a lot more work to be done. But a government must fight the war with all its strength and I do not have any doubts about Fini. His liberal intentions are clear when he made them, and his walk toward liberalism and freedom has been true. Yet still, I will guarantee that I am the equilibrium, or the moderating force in the coalition. In that respect, there is no possibility of escaping this equilibrium of moderation. This must be clear to the outside world.

What will be your government's immediate economic policy goals?

I have never spoken in vain in my life, and I believe that my business success shows it. In the first 100 days of government, if I can help it, it will be necessary to give a helping hand to those who risk, and to those that invest and create jobs. We must move quickly by putting the economy back in motion immediately, and not penalize by imposing high taxes. One of our first priorities will be to control public spending.

One hundred days of the Reagan and Thatcher way? Is this how the model is beginning to emerge?

Not models! But people that I admire, and not Ross Perot which some have mistakenly compared me with. I am not John Wayne in politics. But I would definitely like to have the successes of Thatcher, without having to make the country pay the social costs of those successes.

Here then is the ancient Italian Dream: to make omelette without breaking the eggs. Have not dreams, but the politics of income kept our social peace?

Do you want to ask me, if as prime minister, I would give up the politics of income created by the recent agreement between industry, government and the unions? Professor Martino, my principal economic advisor, who is a liberal of the Friedman school believes in the principle of competition, but he does not preach a war of everyone against everyone.

Agreements are necessary. The goal is not to transform it into a straight jacket that imprisons development, the market and employment. Especially, the young employment which we must defend. I repeat, the agreements with the unions are necessary, as long as they are not transformed into barriers against those that are unemployed, or against those that are looking for jobs for the very first time.

Conducted on April 12, 1994.

AFTERMATH OF THE ITALIAN ELECTIONS
Italy's economic problems can only be resolved by coalition solidarity

Antonio Nicaso

The meltdown begins. After two weeks of infighting and negotiating, Italy is moving towards the formation of a ruling party. Newly-elected leader of Forza Italia, Silvio Berlusconi, and his two partners, Northern League leader Umberto Bossi and National Alliance head Gianfranco Fini, have come to a truce. Bossi, who has once sworn to never govern with the new fascist National Alliance, has softened his resistance to working with Fini. And Fini, for his part, has agreed to work with Bossi in supporting media tycoon Berlusconi as prime minister.

Bossi wanted a promise of change to a federalist system of government and demanded Berlusconi introduce a blind trust, to keep his political agenda separate from his personal and financial holdings. Fini, a nationalist, on the other hand, wants a presidential-type system of government, with direct election of the prime minister.

What has resulted from the lengthy negotiations is a relaxation of positions by all three sides. But has everything been solved? No one would dare to say it with certainty, but behind the scenes, they are all hoping for the best. The optimists are more confident, after face-to-face meetings between Fini and Bossi. Bossi flirted with the losing leftists, provoking both anticipation and distrust. But he has backtracked down the path to the rightist coalition that dominated the March 27-28 parliamentary elections, the first since the Tangentopoli (Bribe City) scandals implicated more than 3000 politicians and businessmen in corruption.

Tangentopoli was the biggest scandal in history, the fallout destroyed the central parties that led Italy since the end of the second World War. What happened to influence the head of the League to return to the Freedom Alliance? Weakness. Over and above the psychological and personal reasons, the fact remains that Bossi realizes that without Berlusconi and Fini, he himself does not have the strength to pursue his immediate political agenda. The only chance Bossi had was to re-enter the Freedom Alliance, but not to go back empty handed, he shifted the priority onto the great big fighting horse of the League: Federalism. This magic word has opened almost all of the doors, and a first political understanding has been formed. Berlusconi has made Bossi aware indirectly that federalism will be one of the main issues of the government program. The same was made with Fini; however, the National Alliance leader proposed a presidential-style system as his demand. The weaving of divergent interests has made a political quilt, that will give future writers of the Constitution many threads to unravel.

At an April 9, 1994 gathering in Pontida, the leader of the Northern League has given Berlusconi free rein. However, Bossi is unyielding on three points: Government, Federalism and Antitrust Law. The Northern League, however, has put its heaviest condition as: "The next government," Bossi shouted, "must be constituent or it will be the last chance for democratic change for the country." The angry federalist added: "If changes don't take place in a short time, just the way we are saying today, we shall find ourselves here in six months, after the government has fallen, to say there are no more possibilities for change. At which time the North will go towards the Northern Republic."

To sum it up, at the Pontida Meetings, sniping attacks on future prime minister Berlusconi have begun. "To the government," Bossi yelled, "we request two mandates: one for the federal constitution and one for the antitrust law and it must be new, at least as new as the American one, which was passed in 1890." Berlusconi replied that he was satisfied with the agreement reached within the Freedom Alliance party. "Now," he said "the future can bring the new economic miracle." And with that he launched his slogan: Less work, more jobs, less government and less taxes.

Afterwards, Berlusconi denied that he was planning to wipe out the top bureaucrats of the first republic and the key people of the ministries and of large public corporations. "I have read also of the vendettas and purification," declared Berlusconi, "I feel as if these are things of another world and far from my spirit and my way of thinking. I believe that everyone can relax."

To sum it up, a Berlusconi government will not create the upheaval in government management, typical in the U.S. system. "As far as I am concerned," Berlusconi told *The G•7 Report,* "I maintain only that we must, all together, roll up our sleeves to rebuild this country of ours. There are so many problems to solve and only with the collaboration of everyone can we think of making it. And whoever thought or wrote of purification and vendettas must, I give you my word as leader, change his mind."

HIGH TECH AND INNOVATION

HIGH TECH AND INNOVATION

These series of themes seem unrelated and forced when considering the titles alone. However, as the decade of the 1990s progressed, it was clear that a true revolution in technology and innovation was taking place simultaneously in many different directions. Jerry Khouri's brilliant piece on "The Political Culture of the Information Highway," set out the issues that the internet was about to raise still in its infant stage of development when this article was written in 1994. This was followed by John Pattison's "Is There too Much Trading in Financial Instruments," already beginning to raise the serious issues around day trading and the spreading equity culture which has made the traditional stock broker a relic of the past in just a few short years.

Regulatory issues captured in "The Three Amigos" and "Barings Finale" centred around the collapse of the "Bankers to the Queen," and the interplay between cultural and regulatory factors that rapidly changing technology is forcing everyone to re-evaluate.

Once again, the auto sector is showcased through "Automotive Sector Revolution" which introduces a new factor in forecasting automotive trends-Quality! Never before has the industry been making such good quality vehicles, and the art of forecasting has come down to understanding how the overall "scrappage" rates are determined.

In "Automotive Design Trends" we use the Detroit Auto Show in presenting the aesthetics that technological advancement is making possible to create.

EARLY SEEDS OF THE INTERNET REVOLUTION

When news of the "internet" in 1993 was rephrased as the "Information Superhighway" very few were in a position to understand and appreciate its immediate impact. When "The Political Culture of the Information Highway" was written in 1994, people were still trying to understand what the effects would be from all of this. Will the information medium be in some way commercialised and controlled by media conglomerates? Or will it remain a non-event, with information flow only of interest and value to academic researchers? As it turns out, the internet has been commercialised, and has both created and attracted most of the venture capital funds available in the U.S. and in Europe to ensure the continuation of its development. To now, commercial transactions have been just a small fraction of overall commerce on the internet, but some sectors such as stock broking and the sex trade have been hit hard.

Intermediaries ranging from the corner retail banks to some of the most exclusive auction houses in major world centres, like Sotheby's and Christie's, have been the most affected to now. Content producers and major media players are still adopting a "wait-and-see" attitude to this new medium, while preferring to bundle their media offering to advertisers that are spanning print, broadcast as well as the internet.

In "Is There too Much Trading of Financial Instruments?" the article asks vital questions in the early years of the decade, which become more and more relevant as we progressed to the new millennium. With portfolio flows growing internationally, and the prominent role in which cross border mergers and acquisitions have come to dominate capital flows in the latter years, new technology used to facilitate this process has left regulators behind. Not only are financial market regulators behind the "black ball," but G7 governments that propose unpopular policies in opposition to the free flow of capital, plant the seeds of crisis and end up working against their own national interests.

W.b.z.V.

THE POLITICAL CULTURE OF THE INFORMATION HIGHWAY
Rapid technological advancement promises to further complicate domestic political relations

Jerry J. Khouri

Language conditions the individual to cultural patterns, argue political sociologists. In other words, the developments of language cannot be disconnected from the environment. In recent years, we have incorporated several words in our modern language. Terms or euphemisms like globalization, competitiveness, total quality management, derecruitment and downsizing. All these personify in some form or another the "new" political and economic age we live in. The phrase "information superhighway" is a culmination of such thinking.

The information highway, much talked about though hitherto undefined, is generally referred to the consolidation of telephone, cable, computer and video technologies or multi-media. Much of the discussion has revolved around technological advancement. Business consortiums have come together to form blocs, each one positioning itself for the 21st century. Undoubtedly, such technological coalescence will be breathtaking in size and impressive in science. It may even be beneficial in areas of research and understanding. However, what is missing in all of this is a serious public discourse about the impact of the information highway on our culture, economy, political institutions and more importantly democracy.

The information highway issue has been loosely dissected into two parts. On the one hand, we have the corporate strategic alliances making up the information empires or multimedia conglomerates. On the other, we have the Internet-- the computer network linking millions of users the world over with access to a computer, a modem and cash. The first is the playground of the big player, where information is commodified, while the latter is for the independent and critical player, where information is disseminated via networks.

Like the Industrial Revolution, the Information Revolution will radically alter our world. The corporate initiative is the introduction of a 500 channel universe and virtual reality. Terms such as virtual classrooms, communities and corporations are being used. This refers to people engaging and "dialoguing" by way of computers rather than face-to-face. The entire spectrum of services, banking, insurance, shopping and travel will be done through television screens. "In fact," writes Heather Menzies, "the highway metaphor is almost a piece of misinformation (and convenient as dis-information), taking us away from understanding the full transformative significance of the changes under way."

Moreover, media as we know it will change. Mass media, the traditional mainstay of information exchange is being shifted. Some speculate, perhaps erroneously, and egregiously, that newspapers, journals and magazines will be obsolete. With the introduction of CD-Roms, online systems and other digital media, magazines are nervous, that inevitably we will be reading the *Financial Times, New York Times, Globe and Mail, Economist* and others on our screens at home.

However, the fact that *Wired* magazine in the United States has been a success and the relaunch of the new media magazine *Shift* in Canada, testify to the possible continuance of traditional magazines, perhaps with some imagination. However, Jeffrey Chester, from the Center for Media Education in Washington, argues that "the paradox of the modern mass media is that all the free speech rights that were intended for individuals and the community are becoming the exclusive property of business."

Nevertheless, can all this be truly healthy to our society? Is all this practical? Do the whiners about such developments have legitimate concerns? Who will control the access to the highway? Who will monitor the carriers? Who controls the costs? Where will free speech and privacy fit into all of this? Such questions and others have not been dealt with.

Victor Navasky, editor of *The Nation*, and on sabbatical at the Harvard Institute of Politics studying journals of opinion and the information age, told the *Boston Globe* last April in an interview, "that a lot more is being written about it (information highway) than it warrants in terms of what we have reason to believe will be its impact-- in the following sense. There are claims that there will be no more libraries in thirty years because there will be no more books because they'll be replaced by databases. I don't see it that way, because I believe the new technological information will not replace the book or the magazine any more than the paperback replaced the hard cover, or movies replaced conversation. It's a new subsidiary right; and if we are smart enough to gain control of it and then provide access to it, it's a way of expanding what we already do and a way or organizing from the bottom up.

With the continuing mania of mergers between media giants and strategically positioned niche companies, the question of control and dominance needs to be addressed. Not one nation has truly articulated a public policy with regards to the information age. While this is partly due to the rapidity of the transformation, it is also a consequence of the massive privatization programs and the permission for companies from different industries, such as cable and telecommunications, to converge.

While privatization in itself is not the problem, it is the manner or lack of preparedness that has exacerbated the issue. Such an important metamorphosis of society, especially when information and knowledge is at issue, is much too important to be left to the whims of the marketplace. Serious cultural and political dimensions, not to mention the concentration of power, have been ignored. The longer they linger the more fractured and dissipated our society will become.

Perhaps a small tale from the media may help. Many independent film makers, consultants, artists and journalists fear that the direction of the highway is headed towards the entertainment industry; where a multitude of movies and a menu of channels are the chore. This then will lead to an illiterate society, thus when the information is required all one needs is a special box with the television set and a credit card, of course. What will happen to books and literature? One leading Canadian writer lamented in the *Globe and Mail*, that "our civilization is falling away from articulation. On the one hand, the airy incoherence of televised lives- and on the other hand, the dense incoherence of academic criticism that has driven fiction to the wall ... the reduction of literature to a commercial unit."

The writer continues by admonishing corporations such as Walt Disney for "deculturing" books. Then concluded that thank god he (Walt Disney) never got his hands on the Tale of Peter Rabbit by Beatrix Potter. Yet the same day in the *New York Times*, it was reported that Britain's Pearson Plc., owner of the *Financial Times*, had bought Software Toolworks Inc. David Veit, chairman of Pearson, was proud about this development and stated that Software's multimedia skills will be used by fashioning the "Tales of Peter Rabbit," into a multimedia program. This story, while minor, exemplifies the sense of ease and quickness by which an important educational tool for children becomes a tool for conglomerates in the name of the information highway.

However, lamenting the negative only clouds the issue. With the advent of the Internet many individuals, independent groups and venture collectives, may, as users, transfer information with ease. Enter the network, and one can be introduced to a multitude of subjects ranging from the politics of Bosnia, Mexico, and East Timor to simple advertisement of a service or product. The net itself is lively, open and relatively democratic. Culturally, such developments encourage community groups the world over to exchange perspectives. There are many nets, and today many cosmopolitan centres are mushrooming with bulletin boards. This is not to say problems do not exist, as individuals can disrupt conversations and dominate it with perfidy.

As nations such as Canada, and the United States begin to think about the entire field of technology, information, education and culture, the development of policy must not exclude consumers and groups who work on the community level. Leaving decisions to a handful of media giants will not be beneficial to civil society. Admittedly, information will, in the future, be a commodity, that is paying for every nugget of information. The issue is what kind of information?

IS THERE TOO MUCH TRADING OF FINANCIAL INSTRUMENTS?

Only co-ordinated attempts at financial market regulation can be successful as global capital & labour mobility increase

John C. Pattison

Governments and the public are asking more questions about trading financial instruments. The analysis of securities trading has usually been academic. When controversial it has been controversy for consenting academics. These debates have concerned such topics as the different ways in which securities markets can be efficient, or alternative hypotheses concerning the determinants of the term structure of interest rates. On the international plane, the ability of purchasing power parity to explain equilibrium prices for foreign exchange rates has been a hardy perennial. Within much of the 20th century these questions were interesting and indeed important to understand how markets work. But it is also the case that governments systematically imposed either barriers to the functioning of these markets - fixed exchange rates, the European exchange rate mechanism, restrictions on bank portfolios, or government dominance of money markets.

Today, markets are getting freer and more competitive on a global basis. With trillions of dollars of mobile funds, governments and some commentators are less sure that they like actively traded competitive markets. This is even more the case for highly indebted countries who are near the limits to their creative financial capabilities. Since there have also been well publicized financial losses, both within financial institutions and for client companies, governments, the press and others have created a lively debate on financial trading.

Arguments Against the Volume of Trading

There are many arguments, both micro and macro. They run the gamut from superficial and populist to complex and academic. What they lack is much analysis or any quantification of the alleged problems.

On the microeconomic front it is hard not to take seriously the thoughts of the eminent Nobel prize winning economist Paul Samuelson. In examining equity markets he poses the question "Are resources overapplied to financial markets?" *(Journal of Portfolio Management, Fall 1994, page 23)*. He goes on to say "To the degree that markets are approximately microefficient, and practitioners are not very successful at timing, why should so many people be necessary to deal in securities?" In a comment that strikes home to most investors he notes that "investors will find it hard to identify the stars from the merely lucky; and after competition makes you pay top dollar for superior service, most investors can eke out for themselves only skimpy excess returns." While he asks appealing questions, much of the solution is found in his article. More and more investors are making investments either with index funds, where they acknowledge that on balance they won't beat the market and more individual investors are going to mutual funds and unit trusts.

In foreign exchange markets, other questions are asked at the micro level. The purchasing-power-parity theory can explain some longer term behaviour, but is irrelevant to any analysis with a horizon of less than five to ten years. In the very short run, the empirical relationships between expected and unexpected currency volatility and exchange rate spreads is helpful to understand options markets, but these reflect day-to-day trading patterns rather than enduring economic fundamentals. Foreign exchange markets tend to overshoot, resulting in major disequilibrium swings. However, at least the foreign exchange markets are pricing the ever-changing values of currencies based upon interest rates, political developments, trade flows and other factors. It is too easily forgotten that the alternative is government management of "fixed" exchange rates, and historically this meant controls over capital flows. Countries risk greater damage to their economies from politically motivated exchange rate management, as opposed to market determined rates. Mexico is a recent example.

As an aside, while more investors have come to this conclusion as portfolio managers, the same analysis and insight has not struck home to many other trading institutions. They believe by their actions that they can create superior trading returns in competitive and efficient markets. In recent years many hedge funds and other institutions have proven this to be false.

What Comprises Trading?

The topic is made more difficult by the task of defining what trading is and putting it into useful categories to be analyzed. One distinction which is made is between hedging and speculation. A hedge trade is a transaction undertaken to offset another position, whereas a speculative trade is one without an offsetting counterpart. But in reality it is difficult to separate many such trades. In many companies, a decision not to trade is a tacit decision to take an underlying risk inherent in the business, for example, from the exchange risk of receivables or payables. Hence, this company is speculating without knowing or appreciating the fact.

Another major distinction is between primary market trading and secondary market trading. Primary markets are those in which new issues of securities are launched usually from a company or government, but sometimes from other sources such as a control block of equities being sold by an investor or the creation of synthetic or derivative securities from other financial assets. Secondary market trading is the trading between "secondary" owners of the securities after the initial distribution of securities has been made. Both should be seen as trades - a 500 million dollar primary underwriting of a new issue and a 5000 dollar purchase of secondary stocks or bonds. Both involve the same issues of risk taking and both give value to corporations, governments and investors. Indeed, here the economic case for active trading is strong as large volumes of trades are necessary to accurately price different, and particularly large volumes of new risks. Since even in a small country there are likely to be thousands of different financial products, liquidity is needed to absorb new issues and active trading of related securities is necessary to price them.

The difference between trading and sales is also blurry. There is a popular idea of trading being between professionals in a zero-sum game, as opposed to securities sales to end-buyers, who hold the securities as investors. But this is also not a robust distinction as investors transact for the same purposes, but with longer time horizons. Large institutional investors are often more akin to traders themselves. The point is that there is a huge, legitimate market for trading financial products that is derived from end investors.

Another trite but significant distinction is between long and short positions. There are many products whose very nature makes it difficult to sell short - mutual funds or unit trusts for example. This is an excellent example where more trading would be socially desirable. If mutual funds could be "shorted" more discipline would be exerted on perpetually poor fund management groups as well as offering investors opportunities to engage in useful trades including hedges.

There are many other useful distinctions, such as those between the market for financial and commodity products themselves and the market for derivatives of these. This is a currently popular source of controversy. However, once again derivatives offer solutions to financial needs which cannot be achieved as efficiently by other means. Derivatives are primarily risk management tools, and it is difficult to understand the widespread negative press which derivatives have received without an equal appreciation for their benefits.

It is difficult to firm up an argument that there is too much trading, when a close look at each type reveals pluses for the economy in terms of pricing financial products efficiently, providing liquidity to absorb new and old issues, providing investment and hedging opportunities.

The Economics of Trading: The Role of Governments

While the supply and demand for trading was discussed earlier, there are some other factors at play. One of the most significant for traders is the role of governments. Leaving aside for the moment the subject of regulation there are many other ways in which governments impact the markets for financial products. One is the supply of government debt which seems on the surface an inexhaustible market. Equally importantly, how governments have intervened in markets, has created imperfections and trading opportunities. When governments target even short run interest rates or exchange rates, they create profit opportunities. These opportunities usually reflect political choices on the part of governments and their preferred dominance over market forces. Since market forces would usually be expected to outlast government attempts at market manipulation, traders have an extra profit opportunity.

However, there are also forces working in the opposite direction which are of great importance to these markets. One is that markets are becoming more efficient, as governments learn to their cost, that fighting global markets is not possible. Second, markets are global today. The implication is that arbitrage quickly eliminates excess profit opportunities where previously local financial markets might have remained mis-priced for longer. As global financial integration continues incrementally, fewer profit opportunities will occur. Another development is innovation in ways to distribute government debt such as tenders, auctions, direct private placements, global issues, cross currency swaps with foreign currency issues, and other techniques which have both created new financing opportunities and revenues for dealers and lowered the returns going to traditional underwriters.

European monetary union would reduce dramatically the opportunities for traders. This would occur not only for currencies, as each nation would lose its separate currency, but also some reduction for government bond market arbitrage as these markets would become a large and diverse ECU market.

Governmental Control & Supervision of Trading

Today, every bank and securities regulator, as well as every insurer of these firms places a primary emphasis on risk management and solvency. However, because these markets are extremely competitive, and in many cases are international, if not global, regulators must balance a natural tendency to over-regulate with concern that the markets will move elsewhere. The Eurodollar and Eurobond market are classic examples, but there are many others. Much of the success of particular foreign products in the London market was due originally to domestic regulation, which had the sole effect of driving business away. Moreover, in these particular markets there were no demonstrable risk management failures. The Bank of England and other UK regulators took over from other domestic regulators in foreign lands. These countries then lost total control of these transactions, as well as employment and tax revenue.

However, achieving a proper balance in regulation is not easy. In many countries, there are still many excessive regulations over trading. These often stem from concern over unsubstantiated risks, risks experienced historically or a desire to protect investors against many possible abuses. Most countries' regulatory systems separate regulations for wholesale, professional or large scale investors, as opposed to retail ones. In the latter case, the rules are often designed with marginal or fraudulent firms in mind.

For wholesale transactions, not only are there statutory controls but some regulators either use their moral suasion to implement a code of conduct, or encourage self-regulatory bodies to do so. In the former case, the Bank of England has implemented quite successfully for many years, The London Code of Conduct. Recent years have seen a proliferation of regulatory standards, codes of conduct, audit manuals and other documents targeted precisely at trading. There could always be a shifting of resources as regulatory needs change, but there is no evidence that trading is under-regulated. The Barings episode does not alter this conclusion. The issues there related more to internal control and corporate governance. While fraud, mis-pricing of positions, hidden transactions and other problems will always exist, regulators cannot solve these and no one has a greater incentive to tackle them than the trading firms themselves.

Final Thoughts

If there was too much trading of particular instruments, such that it undermined the institutions themselves, or trading was excessive relative to underlying economic needs, these financial institutions would have a strong incentive to reduce trading themselves. A regular reading of the *Wall Street Journal* and *Financial Times*, reveals that this is exactly what has happened. Hardly a day goes by where a major institution does not decide to reduce its trading of UK gilts, French OATs, Canadian foreign exchange, Australian dollar Eurobonds and so forth. Equally, trading commences in other products. For those that would like to control these markets either for tax or economic reasons history has no encouragement. Markets are extremely mobile.

The future probably is one with more trading in it. Trading is the key to much of the efficiency of markets, as well as the ability to manage and price risks. As noted earlier, if investors could short sell mutual funds it might be very desirable. Indeed, it is a basic truth that economic history has been continually marked by the growth of trading - new products, new instruments, new risks and new opportunities to manage those risks. Much of economic progress has occurred through creating abilities to spread and share risks. The manufacturer who was at the complete mercy of events would today hedge his output prices, foreign exchange risk, interest rate risk, prices for major inputs such as petroleum or other products and could even enter an insurance contract for political risk. Hence, while the debate over the Tobin tax, derivatives, foreign exchange markets and other issues rage, traded markets will continue to innovate and grow. If roadblocks are put in their way the markets and the people will move.

CORPORATE CULTURES AND REGULATORY ISSUES

This section goes into great details over the Barings affair, and more broader regulatory issues in the 1990s. Leading banking compliance authority, John Pattison, is able to communicate a rare fusion of both theory and practice in this area of growing importance. In "The Three Amigos," an ideally managed environment would address the related topics of corporate governance, financial regulation and internal control. The fact that Barings collapsed in Singapore, one of the best managed financial city centre states from the vantage point of financial regulation, outlines the need for balance. In the Barings case, it was a major shortfall in internal controls and governance that ultimately made a celebrity of trader Nick Leeson.

In the article "Banking and Culture," Barings collapse is once again the focus of how competing cultures within an organisation can lead to disastrous outcomes. The fact that the securities operation in Singapore grew much quicker than the merchant banking unit, resulted in management running with the flow in the expectation of even greater profits.

As technological change mixes with greater globalisation of capital markets, regulatory issues hang in the balance. Any good regulatory system must address both its costs and benefits in determining the socially optimal point at which intervention is desired. These issues, although unnecessarily abstract to many, will only tend to gain in importance with the passage of time.

W.b.z.V.

THE THREE AMIGOS

Governance, Regulation & Internal Control. Is Barings spectacular collapse a prelude to a broader shake-out?

John C. Pattison

This article was written prior to Barings collapse. The first paragraph was originally the following: One of the most important dynamics of financial institutions is being worked out, hidden from public attention by its specialized nature. It is the financial equivalent of $E=mc^2$ in physics. The forces in finance are equally powerful. While this may seem enough to keep conspiracy theorists up-all-night, the reality is quite the reverse. The dynamic is internal control. The question is "How do you control a 200 or 300 billion dollar organization with 50 thousand or more employees?" This question seems to many to be particularly apposite, as financial institutions engage in new businesses such as insurance products, which aren't really new like derivatives, but which are considered risky.

With the shocking events of February 26, 1995 with the announcement of the appointment of administrators for the Barings group, the opening paragraph which I had considered, on reflection, overly dramatic on February 26, seemed reasonable and measured on February 27.

While I intended to focus on the related topics of corporate governance, financial regulation and internal control, I was mindful that many readers would find them individually dull and collectively uninteresting. However, the Barings affair served to highlight all three. The *Financial Times* headlined a story "Why did directors not recognize the risks?" The finance minister of Singapore served to highlight the other two themes:

"Sound regulation is necessary but not sufficient. There is also a need for proper internal controls and procedures on the part of the market participants to ensure that they conduct their futures trading activities prudently."

Corporate governance, regulation and internal control are each necessary for healthy financial institutions. No one alone is sufficient. What is not often recognized, and is a recurrent theme here, is the interdependence of these three. Bad regulation reduces the effectiveness of corporate governance and internal control.

Moreover, no one should look to regulators to stop all failures or to effectively oversee financial institutions. The *Financial Times* on March 4, 1995, posed one view that "regulators were responsible for vetting Barings' control systems; and if they did not know the controls were inadequate they were failing in their jobs." However, in my mind, it correctly went on to say that "it would be a mistake to think foolproof banking regulation is possible or desirable."

Internal control is the process to manage operational risk. When banking risks are considered, most people think of credit risk or market risk such as interest rate or foreign exchange risk exposure. However, lapses in operations can cost tens of millions of dollars on a regular basis and potentially hundreds of millions in extreme situations. As the financial world grows more complex, with derivatives, for example, operational risk management is becoming more important.

Regulators have more than a passing interest and are becoming an ever increasing part of this process. Shareholders, stock exchanges and securities regulators also care vitally and write earnestly about corporate governance. The accounting profession has a significant interest in this topic, as well as risk and liability. The problem of regulators and insurers such as the US Federal Deposit Insurance Corporation (FDIC), is the increasing inter-lock between regulatory power and public insurance schemes, not to mention their concern about their capacity to absorb major financial shocks.

In financial institutions themselves, control is naturally the duty of all management and employees and it must be supervised by a vigilant board. But the challenge is that many employees see their jobs more narrowly, for example, as that of making loans or trading bonds. Many aim for market share or short run profitability over managing operational risk. Many, wrongly, rely on specialized services such as market or credit risk management, compliance or internal audit whose mission is supportive but different from theirs. They are then vulnerable, managing with one hand tied behind their back. Obviously this is a large and complex problem area. What is happening? Where is it going? What is a desirable outcome?

What is Happening?

The action is in three places: the regulators, the insurers and the accountants. The key regulatory change in many countries has been increasing regulations for very detailed compliance requirements at all levels of the organization, up to and including the boards of directors. Often extensive self-assessments must be completed by internal auditors, management must sign off on them, and the Board of Directors must approve the status of compliance. On the surface this is fine and even highly desirable.

This process has gone the furthest in the United States with the Federal Deposit Insurance Corporation Improvement Act. This creates a very substantial and costly workload. One major US bank told me that over a four month period they had put twelve thousand people hours into one such report.
However, even more notably the US leads in micromanagement of financial institutions with approximately 220,000 pages of banking laws, regulations and guidelines. US banking legislation has been a growth industry.

In Canada, the Canada Deposit Insurance Corporation (CDIC) has issued Standards for eight risk areas and requires a detailed self-assessment process, sign-off by internal auditors and management and the passage of a supportive resolution by the Board. Other countries take different approaches. For example, the Bank of England requires the auditors of institutions operating in the United Kingdom to prepare specialized reports on particular risk management issues, for the guidance of the central bank and the expense of the regulated entity. While on the surface this is a seemingly benign initiative, yet simultaneously helpful to the regulator, there is no cost-benefit exercise to support its usefulness either alone or in comparison with other approaches. Nonetheless, as the environment changes it seems to be a way for the Bank of England to deal with current and changing risk issues, without overlaying an annual detailed and more costly comprehensive regulatory regime.

The Canadian CDIC process is highly deceptive. On the one hand the underlying principles are sound. The devil is in the detail. Two problems stand out. There is a requirement for an enormous amount of detail to go to the Board. There is a danger of overloading bank Boards with details that are the legitimate business of management and not directors. The problem is that without a proper balance, the mechanics of CDIC compliance will be a triumph of bureaucratic volume over financial materiality.

The reason this trend is developing is that the regulatory and supervisory apparatus can only go so far to prevent failures of poorly managed institutions. Increasingly, there is a desire to use the corporate governance route - enhancing the supervision by the Board of Directors - to ensure risks are evaluated and that the Board supervises not only management but the outer envelope of risks being taken.

In sympathizing with the challenges of regulators, the problem is that many of the smaller institutions may lack the control infrastructure, control techniques or the specialized monitoring and review functions of the larger banks. Hence, there is a desire to ensure that, at a minimum, the Board carries out these duties. But this is not the correct solution for a huge financial conglomerate. This approach had a natural birth in the US with ten thousand or more banks, but it is not of the same impact, value or consequences elsewhere. Internal control, corporate governance and complying with regulations in today's complex environment is not easy or economical for smaller, marginal institutions.

The second problem is that Board time and that of directors is limited. If more is taken up with the obligatory detail demanded by rote, less time will be available for comprehending the business, the products, the strategy and the macro risk management and control environment that faces them. The legislators and regulators are also coming out with increasingly detailed rules applicable for types of transactions that do not merit, in my mind, the regulatory structure imposed on them. In the United States there is a very detailed structure of control around transactions that carries a much heavier compliance burden than that in almost all other countries. However, there is a trend developing. An example in Canada is the section of the 1992 revisions to the Canadian Bank Act on related party transactions. While this is actually a needed and valuable control, it is implemented in the law in a clumsy, broad brush fashion with some conspicuous illogicalities that detract from its merits. What these related party rules require is approval of individual transactions at the level of a Board committee. This is usually practically impossible or of dubious value for various reasons. The Board Committee could be called upon to opine on the pricing of complex derivative products which is surely not only a job for management, but one where timeliness and skill-sets suggest management over Board.

Another part of the regulatory trend to micromanagement is the international structure of capital requirements approved initially under the auspices of the Bank for International Settlements (BIS). The BIS pulled off a justifiably commendable feat in establishing an international regime for bank capital requirements in the 1980s.

The allocation of risks to this simple two step process does not do justice to the genuine complexities of these risks. This is also regulatory micromanagement. The favourable treatment accorded to domestic and certain international governments, for example, is only partially justified. Worse, these capital standards are an incentive system in themselves, and thereby surreptitiously play their role in allocating financial resources independent of the marketplace. However, the answer is not to scrap them but to improve the process. The accounting profession in many countries has also been concerned with internal control as a factor in the success and failure of many corporations. While the accent may often be on the impact of the control environment on the integrity of financial reporting, the control environment is also vital for operational controls, legal and regulatory compliance and management of business risks. The US Treadway Commission has published a much heralded and quoted framework, for the assessment of the quality of internal controls by companies. This has received international coverage, and the internal control theme has been picked up by the accountancy bodies in other countries as well.

Where is this Trend Going?

There are at least four reasons why there is so much concern with operational risk and internal control, and hence why this trend will likely continue for a while. First, there is huge political fallout from the failures of financial institutions. Second, the systemic costs and risks to the other financial institutions from such failures is unacceptable. Third, risks are perceived to be growing, leading the public, regulators and shareholders to call for a tighter system of internal controls. Fourth, shareholders price equity with a lower price/earnings multiple when earnings are less predictable, for example, because of failures of internal control including risk management failures.

However, the public and political perceptions of these issues, in my view, are faulty. The real problems have not been well articulated. The value of many alternative regulatory approaches have not been properly evaluated or controlled. Many special interests shelter conveniently in the shadows of these misconceptions, since many public interest groups want more regulation. This trend if it continues and if politicized will lead to increasingly invasive regulatory processes, such as those in the US. There is a danger that a new regulation will be seen as the answer to every politician's prayer. This will both lower the international competitiveness of affected markets and lower economic growth through misallocating financial resources. Moreover, the net effect on safety and soundness will be marginal at best.

What Would be a Desirable Outcome?

In my mind, we should divide these issues into two parts, first institutional and shareholders' interests and second, regulatory interests. These two sides are linked in that a solution within a financial institution to the issues of internal control, should go a long way towards solving legitimate regulatory concerns and hence abate some of the current trends.

Shareholders of financial institutions have an interest in lower volatility in earnings, as that will improve price/earnings multiples. To achieve this not only must the financial statements be more insulated from shocks than they were in the 1980s, they must be seen to be protected. Hence shareholders have an interest in:

• good internal control processes;
• high standards of corporate governance at Board and Management level; and
• higher regulatory and insurer Standards that are effective and efficient.

How do we achieve this?

Regulatory and Supervisory Standards

There is no doubt in my mind that the quality of regulation and supervision in all major countries is much better in 1995 than 1985. It is also necessary and appropriate for all financial institutions to do more internal audits and self-assessments, to determine if adequate and effective control and risk management processes are in place to satisfy regulators.

The difficulty is that the risk profiles differ among institutions, and there are alternative ways of achieving the same control objectives. These will also differ between large and small financial institutions. There are compensating controls that achieve control objectives in ways that may differ among institutions. There are elements of rigidity in the FDIC and CDIC process that are not appropriate nor necessary. The challenge is to streamline these to get the maximum value, while allowing the institution to be managed by its board not by inflexible government checklists.

Consequently, the financial industry should embrace the legitimate regulatory objectives of regulators and supervisors. But having done so, regulatory bodies must find less intrusive, more flexible and better targeted ways of achieving these objectives. One method that is used by securities regulators is to set different levels of trip wires for capital, set above the minimum, so that not only is there early warning, but the process that occurs when a wire is tripped captures the attention of management and the Board of the institution. This is low key, unobtrusive, inexpensive, but effective. However, it doesn't deal with the catastrophic risk management events as befell Barings.

Corporate Governance and Internal Control

There are good standards of corporate governance in the United Kingdom's Cadbury Report and similar type reports which have appeared from Canada to Australia - however, you cannot mandate all the responsibilities of a good corporate director - business experience is absolutely necessary. A director of skill and quality is shaped by years of his or her experience with business, financial, economic, regulatory and management challenges. It could also be argued that the corporate governance needs of banks differ from those of manufacturing companies, for example.

The regulatory load on directors can also work against corporate governance as noted earlier. By imposing more and more specific requirements on directors, more time must be taken up by routine matters albeit important ones that could be completed by management. This takes away time for other matters and sets some of the priorities irrespective of the day-to-day challenges facing the particular institution.

If the load becomes too great, as it well might, many good businesspeople will not have the time to shoulder the full demands of an outside financial institution directorship. This will push companies in the direction of the UK model where until recently, you had far more Executive Directors as opposed to outside directors.

Promoting and Substantiating Internal Control

Returning to the opening theme: "How does management create a control environment in a 200 or 300 billion dollar financial organization with 50,000 employees?"
The answer is that you have to work at it with the same dedication and resources that you put into sales or new product launches. Yet many financial institutions have traditionally placed a much lower priority on these issues. What are the steps necessary?

First, companies must be conscious of and promote the control environment - the control culture. The tone is set from the Board and the Chairman and it grows with success stories. It deteriorates when losses and obvious control problems go uncorrected. Second, each member of management must continuously bear full responsibility for frauds, errors, deficiencies, irrecoverable losses and so forth. There must be accountability, not delegation to audit or internal control. The outcome of both steps will be a significant return on investment. Large institutions suffer many avoidable losses through control weaknesses. Good corporate governance and good control probably have a return on equity that is in double digits.

To some extent, some companies have an attitude problem with internal control! They see control losses as a salesman sees traffic infractions, merely as a cost of doing business. Such an organization is building problems for the future. This is particularly the case if such a corporate culture is tolerated at Board level. This then becomes a corporate governance failure. The link between the two is transparency of management processes and frequent board review of and contact with senior staff. Fortunately, in the better managed financial institutions this is something which does occur frequently.

Some Concluding Thoughts

What conclusions can be reached on the importance of corporate governance, regulation and internal control in safeguarding the health of financial institutions? First, expect and encourage high performance from your Board and management but don't have regulators tie one hand behind their back with inflexible programs. This is a high priority item for bank lobbying in several countries. In my view, the better and safer regulatory environments are those which place greater emphasis on supervision over regulation. Moreover, those regulators who have broader powers, such as the Bank of England, can better tailor their resources and priorities to their current, but changing assessments of risks, than those regulators encumbered with a greater volume of laws and regulations.

Second, financial institutions must embrace the legitimate goals of regulators and supervisors, if for no other reason than to reduce the cost of failing companies, and to reduce the threat of more intrusive regulations. All sides must seek more efficient and effective regulatory processes. Yet in reality both the financial institutions and regulators focus most on the status quo.

Third, in response to this challenge, legislators must be more market sensitive and creative in allowing alternative ways to achieve legitimate control objectives. The 220 thousand pages of banking law in the US is obviously excessive.

Fourth, it is vital to create a good internal control environment starting at the top. The travelling salesman syndrome encapsulates a very dangerous attitude. However, it has probably been caused at least in part by the sheer volume of regulation. Less can be more in the financial regulatory field for the good reason that scarce internal control resources must be dedicated to genuine risks, rather than responding in a bureaucratic fashion to a large catalogue of risks.

Comparative analysis of different international regulatory regimes supports this view. The Bank of England is a good example of a balanced and cost effective regulatory regime as noted above. Singapore is also a good example. It is regrettable that the Barings episode occurred on their territory, but it says less about these regulatory bodies than it does about internal control exigencies in small to medium size financial institutions. It also reinforces my earlier theme that strong and efficient practices must simultaneously exist in governance, regulation and internal control.

BANKING & CULTURE
Barings Collapse Spotlights Managerial Issues

John C. Pattison

The trend towards the liberalization of entry barriers to financial services has given rise to significant cultural challenges to the management of financial institutions. One set of issues pertains to the interface between investment banking and commercial banking. The differences in corporate cultures between these two types of organizations are factors which feature in many articles on this topic, without necessarily going into sufficient depth to understand the issues.

These issues relate not only to marketing and management, as commonly conceived, but also to matters of internal control. One conclusion which is becoming increasingly clear is that the two cultures presented as two solitudes, which was true in the 1980s, is no longer as valid. Indeed, in many leading firms, commercial and investment banking cultures are supporting one another. Rather than being a barrier to change, the two can work together using the innate strengths of both to make the combined firm better and stronger. What are the concrete signs of these issues? Are there corporate problems which have their origins in corporate cultures, or is there merely an identification problem in isolating different business influences which interact simultaneously? For example, is the difference between compensation systems a cultural factor or merely a human resources failure, which can be corrected once it is correctly identified?

Corporate Culture as Real and Living

A corporate culture is defined by the values, assumptions, attitudes, beliefs and expectations of the members of a group. It is often stated in the literature, that the above characteristics of a corporate culture are shared by all employees. However, the degree to which the characteristics of a corporate culture exist in individual employees, or alternatively that the shared nature of the characteristics is revealed in inter-active preferences, is best viewed as less a definition than a further description or analysis of the culture. The reason for this distinction is particularly important in investment banking, as well as in certain other organizational forms, particularly partnerships. In investment banking, there are elements of strong individualism, where large numbers of employees work more for themselves than for corporate goals. The issue is aligning and controlling them. It seems likely, based upon published reports, that some significant elements of cultural failure may have played a part in the failure of Barings. *Euromoney (March 1995)* reported that "strife between the merchant bank and the securities operation, allowed not only Leeson's unit but all the Asian derivatives operations to grow their businesses too fast, without proper supervision." However, it is important not to confuse general management weaknesses with cultural schisms.

To identify the existence of the problems after the fact is relatively simple. The experience in most major capital markets where there is an overlap between commercial banks and investment banks has exhibited a pattern, albeit one with a trend as well. Corporate finance staff, securities salespeople and traders have voted with their feet. In the United Kingdom, Switzerland, Australia, Canada, Germany and elsewhere these staff members changed jobs in conspicuous fashions, in some cases in teams of up to ten or more. Although there is a two way flow, in the 1980s the pattern showed staff more frequently leaving commercial banks and joining investment banks. The reverse flow was small and where it existed, it was in favour of those commercial banks which have clearly repositioned themselves as investment banks. However, in the 1990s with commercial banks repositioning themselves in investment banking markets, the cultural variables are just as real, but now cultural and performance weaknesses in investment banks are leading to a two-way flow that better illustrates some of the cultural factors.

Although compensation issues, different bonus arrangements, "golden hello's" and other financial factors figure in employee mobility for investment bankers rather than commercial bankers, there are a large number of other factors which are regularly involved. These are regularly commented upon in the press and include frequent corporate reorganizations in commercial banking; the organizational separation of functions within a commercial bank which are integral to investment banking such as treasury, risk management, private banking, settlements and operations facilities; the degree of perceived commitment to excellence often in particular specialties or areas of the business; the extent of authority delegated to investment bankers in commercial banks including risk management; uncertainty over the influence of investment bankers in the commercial bank; the perception of narrowed career prospects for investment bankers in a commercial bank; style of management; and the feeling that the investment banking strategies of commercial banks are uncertain and undeveloped.

Investment Banking Culture

The management literature on corporate culture often follows a number of lines of analysis which are of limited value in studying investment banking. One is the focus on the role of top management as a, or the, key determinant in the culture. My view, having managed trading and investment banking activities in the U.K. and Canada, is that top management is vital for two things. First, creating the control environment. Second, the senior executive of an investment bank must be like the madame in a house of ill repute. He or she must create the environment where clients are well served. However, it is not possible to participate in, or oversee, or review each transaction. The critical factor is the need for large numbers of staff with highly specialized skills to pursue them in a solitary fashion, such as traders or salespeople, or in small dedicated groups. Senior management's role, while important, is significant mainly in supporting and shaping the culture or environment, as well as the control structure. A second erroneous or misleading factor in the literature is the accent on shared beliefs. Unlike other industries the shared beliefs, such as they are, pertain less to macro or industry specific factors, but rather to the behavioural psychology of these staff. The cultural factors to be analyzed below, provide a better framework for an understanding of this industry. They fit into two categories: factors intrinsic to the business, and factors intrinsic to the staff in the industry.

Business Factors in Investment Banking Culture

Ritual

Rituals are central to all corporate life, culture and organizations, whether or not they are recognized as rituals. In commercial banking, rituals are internal to the firm. These rituals historically stemmed from the hierarchical structure and the layered, separable nature of decision making in a large complex organization, combined with the long periods of service which have characterized commercial bankers and have reinforced rituals. In an investment bank, ritual and protocol are largely external to the firm and originate in the characteristics and operations of the marketplace (bond, foreign exchange, money market, stock markets, commodities, mergers and acquisitions and so forth). Employees often develop greater loyalty to their market than to their employer, particularly since mobility is high and their long term security is seen as coming from the market. Rather than having and forming corporate rituals, the necessities of the marketplace dictate that a corporation imports these "rituals" with the specialized staff it hires. This then raises the probability that cultures will clash.

Separability and Bonding

In a commercial bank many of the key activities are not only separable, but the size of the organization and prudential requirements of credit control and market risk management, have led to divisional structures with segmented communications. These have created regimental-like units which may not pull together well as a team.

An investment bank has important similarities to this structure and one important difference. The similarities are that an investment bank has a number of distinct and separable functions. However, the profitable execution of transactions requires that these groups work in a connected fashion and become bonded together. An example may be appropriate. In underwriting a stock or bond, the marketing and syndicate arms must be realistic about the structure and pricing of the transaction which it is buying. The traders must validate these prices in the marketplace and the salesmen must have end-buyers at these legitimate market prices. The settlements area must perform payments and deliveries on time without failure, which in this business are sufficiently costly to undermine the entire operation. For profitability, all must work together simultaneously without failure. This is unlike, for example, the credit area of a bank which could quite rightly turn down a transaction for prudential reasons, in what may be perceived as being in isolation from other aspects of the transaction or the organization.

There is an implication of this distinction which is extremely important, as it is at the heart of successful and unsuccessful corporate cultures in investment banking. In all cases in investment banks, the dynamic tensions among the working groups is high because they all have fundamental price conflicts with one another. A salesman, for example, has a different interest in the quoted prices from a trader or marketing person, and moreover, he will distrust their motives. In successful companies these dynamic tensions are not only controlled, but the resultant conflicts are managed so that the underlying economic factors guiding each group are harnessed to benefit the company. In unsuccessful investment banks these tensions tear apart the key units, particularly where management places more emphasis on one part of the company than another, thereby ultimately encouraging one or more groups to change employers in this environment.

Control

Investment banks are required to delegate considerable authorities to individuals. These are carefully managed by the most senior officers of the firm, who should know at all times what their positions were and what their risk was. As a consequence, the risk exposure can be changed quickly. Being an opportunistic industry, limits, controls and authorities are managed in an opportunistic manner, and changed very quickly. This is not a bad thing. In fact, this can be a prudent approach. This is a very different situation from that in a large commercial bank, where controls have historically been implemented via rules and prohibitions designed prudentially, to reduce the decision making ability of large numbers of employees to prevent loan losses and defalcations. Nonetheless, investment banks are managed by a more direct, more frequent hands-on alteration of their authorities and transactions by the highest levels of management.

"Partnership Culture"

Investment banks have evolved from partnerships. This has had an enormous impact on their cultures, and indeed, I believe that a partnership is the ideal form of a risk-taking, betting-gambling type organization were it not for two factors: the need for large scale capital in today's world-wide markets, and the related need to deal only with secure, "undoubted" counter-parties in large transactions.

Partners are jointly and severally liable for their obligations. As a consequence, the awareness of their personal liability and responsibility for risk is high, and the connectedness of different activities is likewise high as the group is bonded together with a common interest in their personal financial well-being. Partnerships encourage the observation of one anothers' work, risk-taking and contribution. By contrast, there remains an asymmetry in the traditional corporate form of such organizations, as employees can be positively motivated by remuneration schemes which share the benefits on the upside, however, there is little that can be done to create the sharing of the risk on the downside. It is one of the challenges of management to create a synthetic culture more like a partnership for investment banking. Examples are emerging and warrant further observation.

Client-Employee Links

Investment bank employees usually have a unique one-to-one relationship with their clients. From the point of view of clients, a high level of service and advice can be extremely profitable to an individual or a corporation. The employee being remunerated by results can sometimes have his primary loyalty to the customer, his secondary loyalty to his marketplace and only his tertiary loyalty to his firm. Therefore, he will work hard for the client relationship. Should the employee change employer, in many cases he will take his clients with him. Therefore, in hiring an employee, you are also buying a client list and ensuring that the employee can start to produce income within a shorter period than would otherwise be the case.

Personal and Psychological Factors in Investment Banking Culture

The Nature of Ambition

Investment bankers are at least as ambitious as any other employee. However, this ambition is usually very heavily weighted in terms of remuneration, rather than hierarchy. The independent nature of many of the individual jobs, the remuneration, and the less desirable culture of management militate against these employees seeking a place higher up the organization. Nonetheless, within the culture of an investment bank, ambition for larger trading limits and position taking ability, and for the ability to be authorized to deal with clients on behalf of the firm in a marketing context are extremely important, although there is less interest in titles and non-financial perquisites that come with promotion in other activities. However, when the investment banking culture comes in contact with a commercial banking culture, these latter factors can re-assert themselves in a potentially non-benign fashion, as they become visible totems of esteem in a more complex organization which many of these employees may not fully understand, and which is perceived as threatening or undermining their relative status or importance. This is particularly difficult where the differences arise over legitimately contested matters of risk management which affect the ability to do the job.

In its natural form there is another fashion in which ambition is seen as having an important influence on the culture in an investment bank. Since many of the employees are highly paid, while there is no hierarchical title structure to record prominence that is both visible and comparable within the industry, considerable prestige is placed on the public indicators of corporate achievements. Since many firms are part of conglomerates, some are partnerships and many have methods of sheltering income from tax, reported profitability is not a useful or reliable standard of inter-firm comparison. Instead, there is an over-emphasis on visible forms of comparative standings which are generally market share information in the form of rankings, number of major deals and so forth.

The prominence which these rankings has assumed has had a number of important cultural impacts on the industry. First, many employees having achieved financial success, strongly desire to work for a firm that is perceived to be moving up in the business, or is at, or near the top at the present time. As a consequence, when a firm becomes less successful, or for prudential reasons becomes more cautious, there is a very real threat of losing key employees. Second, concern with the visible signs of firm success, which are essentially market share statistics, often leads to non-profit maximizing behaviour by the firm itself.

Communications

One of the biggest cultural gaps between investment bankers and commercial bankers concerns the forms of communications. In investment banking, there is a clear preference for speed, for verbal communications over written correspondence. Where written, the preference is for electronic or facsimile messages rather than memorandum or telex. Because of the need for urgency there is less concern with form and protocol than in commercial banks. This can lead to cultural conflicts in many predictable ways. It can also lead to inaccuracies and misunderstandings.

An extension of this is that the smaller and older investment banks have a high degree of intolerance for paperwork and routine forms. This is partly because of the partnership-type checks and balances. It reduces overhead and partly because products and markets change so frequently that written documents have rapid irrelevance. In addition, partners knowing one another well, found that verbal communications resulted in few misunderstandings. However, as these smaller partnerships become exposed to global competitive and market factors, they may fail spectacularly, as their control environment is not up to the task of the risks they are assuming.

The Management of Cultural Change in Investment Banking

The above discussion of the investment banking culture provides detailed reasons to carefully manage both culture and cultural change. A basic framework for action must include the following factors. First, the fact that ritual and much of the culture is external to the individual firm implies that management must not be isolated or remote. Management must become part of the staff and be located in the heart of the trading, capital markets or related areas. By doing so, the necessitates of rapid communication and good risk management are assisted, and management submerses itself in the heart of the cultural activity. While a large number of major firms do this, most observers would credit the reason to the speed of markets, communications or risk management, rather than culture. The cultural aspects must not be underestimated.

Second, the dynamic tensions among the interdependent groups are an extremely dangerous factor, even though they are indispensable. In order to manage this balance, management must give equal and/or fair weight, corporate influence on decision-making, directorships and attention to each group. While attention is vital, a disproportionate amount of management favour could be harmful. Should some key groups have notable deficiencies, the word should be spread that the problems are being addressed quickly. This is for two reasons. First, so that other areas need not fear that their profitability and hence remuneration will suffer for long, due to gaps elsewhere in the company. Second, so that extra staff, attention, salaries and so forth that are used to correct the situation, not be seen as favouritism by those who are not close to the problem.

Third, the culture must be seeded thoughtfully and carefully with profitability ritual, tokens and other elements rather than market share, league tables and related targets. Although some of the reasons for this concern were noted earlier, an additional one is continuity. Non-profit maximizing behaviour will generate its own dissatisfactions and cause undue mobility, even if the management was willing to tolerate such a situation only in the short run.

Fourth, excellence in administrative management will take the risk management, administrative and communications load from staff who are poor at it to begin with. Moreover, administration is often labeled unfairly as bureaucracy. This can be a divisive factor, while its proper handling will make the firm run much better than if carried on by the investment banking specialists.

Fifth, to the extent possible, more than one staff member should get to know each client well. Electronic means of storing information should allow client and other information to be available for employees' use without being available in a fashion that is easily transportable. This is less a cultural factor than a method of dealing with the mobility of this culture. Finally, these two cultures are not mutually exclusive or necessarily competitive. A firm that integrates the two successfully will easily succeed over firms dominated only by one culture.

BARINGS FINALE
Can the File be Closed?

John C. Pattison

The failure of Barings must bring out many mixed emotions to those in the financial industry, not to mention regulators and customers of banks and securities firms. Yet at its root it appears very simple. The July 18, 1995 Report of the Board of Banking Supervision Inquiry into the Circumstances of the Collapse of Barings described the facts quite well: "A material failure in the management, financial and operating controls of Barings enabled massive unauthorized positions on exchanges to be established without detection". The report went on to say that "these control failings were in the Singapore, London and Tokyo offices of Barings and ranged from the failure of high level group management controls ... through several organizational units and business functions, to day-to-day operating controls, such as those over the disbursement of funds."

In reality, the Barings problem was not kaleidoscopic, but rather simple and narrow at its origin. The collapse was due to the unauthorized trading of one person, together with a lack of segregation of duties in that one office. This lack of segregation both allowed the trading to occur and prevented it from being detected in a timely manner. However, there were many warning signals that went unheeded, and the damage need not have been as severe as it was.

The Report by the Board of Banking Supervision is fascinating and contains more detail than most readers require. However, it is incomplete. Vital information from Singapore was not available, hence there may ultimately be more to the story than has been revealed. In particular, it appears likely that more people in Singapore may have been aware of the false accounting.

The true significance of the Barings failure lies elsewhere. Partly, this is from the shock value. Like the Titanic it should not be surprising that banks, like ships, sink. In both cases the interest is in the speed of their going. Bank supervisors, like marine rescuers, deal best with situations of slow decline. The most interesting part of the Barings affair is in the lessons, and if not the lessons, the future reactions by governments, central banks and bank supervisors. There are no new lessons for management in the affair. Nonetheless, some old lessons are given embellishment for the age of derivatives and global institutions, and these are worth consideration by bank management and boards of directors.

What should Bank Supervisors Do?

The Report contains a detailed analysis of the perambulations of the Bank of England and to a lesser extent, Securities and Futures Authority regulators among others. There are some lessons sometimes clarified by hindsight. Even where a Bank of England regulator's actions are questioned, it remains likely from the analysis that he had a reasoned approach to his actions, even if they should have been more transparent to his supervisors. Regrettably, the facts on which his analysis was based were faulty. The big question is what could the regulators have done to prevent the failure of Barings? In my view, it would not only be wholly unrealistic to expect the Bank of England to have identified the problem, but a system that led to this conclusion would create the wrong mix of managerial-governmental and consumer incentives. Why is this the case?

First, consider the nature of the problem and its cover up. The root cause was identified by management, highlighted by the internal audit, acknowledged by more senior management, but evidently not thought important enough to rectify. The external auditors caught a glimpse of a piece of the puzzle. If all of this talent which had strong personal and corporate incentives to deal with the problem could not do so, how could the Bank of England staff who had collective responsibility for a large number of banks?

However, the affair does raise the issue of what bank supervisors can do. Could the world's best central bank or bank supervisor have prevented the fall of Barings? If the answer was "yes," the question must also be asked "at what price?" and "would such a regime be desirable?" However, the Barings failure could still leave a valuable legacy if it sheds light on the limits to supervisory efficacy.

My own view is that there are only three functions which a bank supervisor can provide to enhance safety and soundness. First, for an institution in slow or progressive decline, a bank supervisor can take many constructive steps to mitigate the damages or the contagion, or can require management to inject new capital, change accounting practices, alter business practices, improve certain controls, inject new management and so forth. The Bank of England has had a commendable history in dealing in this way. In fact, one reason for the relative success of the Bank of England is that the Banking Act of 1987, gives enormous range to the Bank to opine on such matters in an authoritative way. Supervisors in other countries are often not as fortunate because of their legislation.

Second, a supervisor can promote through various alternative techniques an understanding of the minimum acceptable internal control and risk management standards. In other words, practice safe banking. There are a number of techniques available in different countries and including the Section 39 reports required by the Bank of England. However, as to optimum techniques there is curiously little light to be shed on an area in which there is enormous international experience. One reason is that central banks and bank supervisors act on a stage with high standards of confidentiality. There is much to be learned about process, but nobody in a position to do so.

The third function which a bank supervisor (as well as management) can do is what is called in the securities industry as "Know your Client." Both the Bank and Barings thought of the arbitrage business in Singapore as being essentially riskless, yet conversely, believed it to be highly profitable. What is feasible is for the bank supervisor to understand the basic financial variables, such as source and use of funds, profitability, balance sheet breakdown and so forth. If these seem mutually inconsistent, as they were in the case of Barings, both supervisors and management should press until they receive an answer that is satisfactory to them. Earlier, it was stated that it might just be possible for a bank supervisor or central bank to prevent a Barings type failure. The solution would be a strong dose of points two and three, that is, strongly promote internal control as a duty of officers and directors and require intensive "know your client" information and analysis by regulators. One element of Barings that is relevant to regulators and those concerned with public policy in this area is that

Barings, in the scheme of things, was a small bank. To be a global player in complex markets requires greater scale both as to capital, and so that there is a greater chance that the correlation in risks works in your favour.

What are the Lessons for Management?

Internal control is as vital to financial institutions as control systems are to aircraft. Unfortunately, for some banks such as Barings, the internal control framework did not receive the attention it deserved. However, the results are unpredictable. Most control systems, especially those on aircraft, are designed for overlapping coverage and built-in redundancy, hoping that the extra control leverage, while vital, will not be needed. Hence, control failures do not automatically subject the firm or aircraft to catastrophic failure. What they do is shift the probabilities and create a significant statistical probability of failure where it was small previously. Hence, without costly events, many firms under-invest in control. In the Barings case, the multiple control failures coincided with a situation where a trader was predisposed to unauthorized dealing, with predictable and regrettable results.

Three interesting and important managerial findings from Barings are worth noting. First, many international financial institutions rely on a matrix structure where employees could report on a product line basis to one manager, for marketing management to another, and to another manager for local office reasons. This structure compounded the problems at Barings. As one senior Barings officer was reported to have said in the report, "Barings has tended to be unstructured about reporting lines in any case over the years." The Report in noting that matrix management is not unusual does say that "a cornerstone of its effectiveness is the integrity and reliability of internal controls at the local office level."

Second, why didn't anyone heed the many warning signs? What Barings illustrated is that a framework and systems of internal controls are necessary but not sufficient conditions for success. What is also required is a clear communications process for all managers. Having determined what messages are important, but with the probabilities of adverse consequences being unknown, how do these messages rise above the background noise which is often heavy and competitive in corporate communications channels? Barings illustrates as much as anything, that this needs thoughtful attention.

Third, corporate culture is itself a palpable variable in corporate success or lack thereof. The Report is full of references to the very different cultures of Baring Brothers & Co., Limited and Barings Securities Limited. As a result, it is also not surprising that the control culture was not strong in the combined organization even though some individuals, such as the internal auditors and some others, did identify and communicate the weaknesses.

Where do we go from here?

There is much to digest in the Report of the Board of Banking Supervision. There is much for management, auditors and regulators to reflect upon. What should be addressed by all parties is a continual review of the effectiveness of processes; what works and what doesn't work. As a familiar military motto states "The price of peace is eternal vigilance."

The unknown question is what impact the Barings failure will have on banking and securities regulators? It is too early to tell. Moreover, banking and securities regulators in many parts of the world do not work as closely together as they need to do, and the activities of global institutions may be unevenly regulated. Indeed, this reverts back to my earlier point. It would be totally wrong to expect regulators to stop failures. That job rests with management and the boards of directors that appoint management. However, governments often create incentives to take greater risks than markets would allow. An example is deposit insurance, although this was not a factor in Barings, it is often central to funding excessive risk taking in other institutions. What is needed is more public light shed upon the comparative techniques of bank supervision. We have the capability of learning from extremely valuable cross country experience, but the mechanisms are not in place to do so.

THE END OF CYCLES AND THE RISE TO QUALITY

All of a sudden, there were no more boom-bust cycles in the automotive sector. It seems that the challenge of cyclical management in auto production has come down to an art form in the 1990s. Issues such as quality, leasing and incentive programs have acted to remove the cyclicality. Moreover, supply management has now become achievable, whereas in the 1970s and the 1980s, a consumer buying boom was met with bringing on new capacity, only to exacerbate the downturn when the new production came on stream two to three years later. This unco-ordinated attempt to meet growing demand for cars has been relegated to history by all producers.

In "The Art of Automotive Sales Forecasting," Dennis DesRosiers submits that increasing quality levels in vehicles produced has made the auto sales forecaster's life more difficult. For the first time, the auto cycle now must contend with higher quality vehicles that carry more "equity" for all consumers than they ever had in recent history. Consequently, consumers have the option now to put off buying a new car for many more years. Not only this, but the used car market has exploded upwards with the increasing quality of all cars that are now produced.

W.b.z.V.

AUTOMOTIVE SECTOR REVOLUTION
Living Without Cycles

Dennis DesRosiers

I just finished reading Peter Lynch's book "Beat the Street." Peter was the investment manager for the Fidelity Magellan Fund, one of the most successful equity mutual funds in the US between 1977, when he took over the Fund, and 1990 when he left. In his book there is a chapter on playing what Peter calls "the cyclical auto stocks." I have a lot of respect for his advice, and he certainly has been more successful playing the market than I will ever be, but the traditional view of the auto sector stocks as "cyclical" may now be flawed.

To be sure, the automotive market has always been cyclical and many investors have been able to do very well by understanding the auto cycle and by timing their entry into, and their exit from the market. However, the auto market has a cyclical history for very technical reasons. On the upside of the market, consumers would buy a large volume of new vehicles over a three to five year period. This created a very positive atmosphere in the economy. The media reported these healthy sales increases, which created a positive psychological reaction with consumers. "Since all these people are buying cars maybe I should buy a car," and sure enough, many consumers did purchase. Auto and auto parts production boomed during these up cycles which created a large volume of jobs both directly and indirectly in the economy. As employment grew, even more consumers bought new vehicles, further adding to the upside.

But eventually the market peaked, and for many very valid reasons, consumers would start to buy fewer vehicles. Perhaps the economy turned sour. Maybe interest rates went up. There has also been exogenous shocks like the energy crisis. But, for whatever reason, consumers stopped buying as many vehicles. However, the downside of the auto markets has proven to be very slippery. Now the media is negative, consumers are scared, and the market snowballs downhill, gaining momentum as it collapses. Some of these down cycles have been as long as three or four years. But consumers could once only delay their purchase of a new or newer vehicle for so long. Eventually they had to come back into the market and the "cycle" started all over. Why do consumers come back?

When consumers purchase a vehicle they are in essence purchasing access to a certain number of kilometres of transportation. The same is true with businesses and their vehicle purchases. The number of kilometres the consumer will drive a vehicle before they trade for a new or newer vehicle varies widely. If they buy a ten year old rust bucket they may only get another 30-50,000 kms. If they buy a small inexpensive new car, it may be driven for 150-200,000 kms. Not necessarily by the first owner, but it will be driven that distance over its life. If they purchase a very high quality mid size car, the vehicle may last for 200-250,000 kms. Some classics, like the Toyota Camry or Buick LeSabre can last up to 300,000 kms.

Not all vehicles wear out. Many vehicles are taken off the road after very little use if the vehicle is in an accident. Others may be retired because of expensive repairs such as an engine job or transmission job. Even a minor accident can take an older vehicle off the road since it may not be worth repairing. The average vehicle (taking accidents into account) runs for between 200,000 and 250,000 kilometres. Even some one to five year old vehicles are scrapped each year, but the majority of vehicles come off the road after they are ten years old.

During a downturn, when all the economic factors are negative, consumers keep their existing vehicle instead of buying a new vehicle. That is one of the reasons the market is cyclical. Scrappage also slows somewhat during different economic times as some consumers just cannot afford to move to a newer vehicle. When the economic and other factors are positively aligned, consumers quickly come back into the market to renew the kilometres available for use in their vehicles. Again, this adds to the cyclicality of the market.

Peter Lynch and his associates, and dozens of auto analysts, have studied these cycles in depth. They traditionally have been very good at understanding these cycles and picking the auto stocks. But I believe we are exiting the era of high cyclicality in the auto sector and entering an entirely new era of relatively stable growth with very little cyclical movement in the markets. An era that Peter Lynch and many of the other stock market guru's have yet to fully understand. There are currently a long list of variables, issues and supply and demand management tools available, which will take much of the cyclicality out of the auto sector. They would include the following:

- the high quality of vehicles
- the affordability issue/high consumer debt
- technology
- demographic issues
- leasing
- interest rates
- the use of incentive programs
- retention programs
- three shift production schedules

Now that vehicles are so well built, consumers can delay their entry into the market. In the past, if they delayed their vehicle, quality and integrity deteriorated rapidly and after a few years they had no choice but to explode back into the market. Many of the vehicles just could not meet their transportation needs. This explosion back into the market added to the cyclicality of the auto sector. Now, the consumer is driving a high quality vehicle, they can come back at their own speed and this reduces cyclicality.

In the past, vehicle prices, in real terms, were falling. Today, new vehicle prices, relative to after tax income, have never been higher. Furthermore, consumers are carrying very high levels of debt, and are facing new demands for their money including home renovations, electronic equipment and retirement savings. During past cycles, when their debt levels were low and vehicle prices were more affordable, they could re-enter the market very quickly. Today, they struggle to buy a vehicle and re-enter the market very slowly. The affordability problem is therefore a major contributor to reduced cyclicality.

Today, there is less new additional technology on new vehicles. During the 60's and 70's, consumers were faced with a dazzling display of new technology each year that encouraged them to re-enter the market quickly. There is less reason to buy a new vehicle today, simply due to fewer and more marginal improvements in technology.

Looking at demographics in Canada and in the U.S., the baby boomers reaching their driving age and starting families, in addition to the rapid entry of women into the labour force during the 1960's and 1970's added to the upside of each cycle. Now, boomers already own their vehicles. Many already own more than one. They simply have to replace them, which also makes the sector less cyclical. On the supply and demand management side of the auto sector, there are now many more "tools" at the industry's disposal. For instance, in the past, the industry built entirely new plants to meet new demand. These plants had to be kept operating at high levels of capacity, whether the market for the vehicles existed or not. Therefore, the industry did everything possible to keep sales high as markets softened. The vehicle companies were very guilty of overheating the market to support their factories. A good example of this is the millions of daily rental program cars sold through the late 1980's which completely disrupted the market.These incentives added to cyclicality, since they drew sales forward into current production years. This overheating of the market eventually led to a stronger decline in sales, when the market could no longer support higher sales. Thus, when sales collapsed, they really collapsed. Today, the production systems are very different. Many of our factories now use overtime and run three shift operations to produce the extra vehicles needed when demand is strong. Using these new production tools allows the vehicle companies to better manage their supply of vehicles.

To be sure, the auto sector still uses a number of incentive programs to move specific makes and models. But even here, they have become much more adept at managing demand. One of the most common incentives is the setting of residual values in leases. By setting a high residual value in a lease, the monthly payment on the vehicle is reduced and consumers are better able to purchase a vehicle. This type of incentive can be targeted to specific vehicles or to specific areas of the country. Even to specific dealerships. There are downside risks to higher residuals which should not be ignored, but this type of incentive can be an effective tool to manage demand and reduce the cyclicality of the market. Leasing reduces cyclicality because every person that utilizes a lease has their own two to four year cycle that exists independent of market forces. When the lease ends, they either buy their vehicle out or move into a new lease. In either case, cyclicality is significantly reduced.

Even the Federal Reserve and the Bank of Canada seem to be micro managing interest rates to the auto industry's benefit. During 1994, the auto market was beginning to explode so interest rates were increased a number of times starting in January 1995. This cooled-off what was beginning to become an overheated auto market in the US and very effectively helped reduce the cyclicality of the auto sector.

I believe the shape of the demand curve in the North American auto sector has changed dramatically. The decline in sales following the 1988 peak has been longer than past downturns, but it has not been as deep. Whereas the trough in 1982 that followed the peak in sales in 1978 represented a 30 percent decline, sales have dropped only 17.8 percent from the peak in 1988 to the trough in 1991. And whereas sales leaped 51.1 percent from the 1982 trough to the 1988 peak, from the 1991 trough to the 1994 peak, sales increased by a more modest 19.4 percent. Had sales followed earlier patterns of cyclicality we would all be enjoying sales in excess of 19 million units right now! Of course, this would have been followed by sales dropping back to 15 million units around 2001, but that would just be before the launch of a new surge in sales that would crack 20 million units sometime past 2005.

What we are seeing instead, are sales that will continue to sputter around 16.5 to 17.5 million units per year into the next century in Canada. Sales will begin to match their long-term demand curve much more closely. There will be annual fluctuations — no industry is immune to that — but vehicle manufacturers and industry watchers will find these fluctuations much more stable than before. This will be good for the industry, since it will make demand forecasting much more reliable. This in turn, will help manufacturers and their suppliers plan materials requirements more effectively, bringing greater short-term stability in the prices they pay for resources.

For stock market analysts, the more stable demand, more predictable production requirements and more stable resource costs will be the result. The auto industry will move from being cyclical and appealing to speculators, to a mature, stable growth industry with appeal among value-oriented investors. For Mr. Lynch, the formula which helped him sell books on cyclicals will no longer apply in the auto industry.

THE ART OF AUTOMOTIVE SALES FORECASTING
Shapes, Patterns & Cycles

Dennis DesRosiers

I read a very interesting article in the *Financial Times* of London related to the confusion amongst US auto industry analysts, as to the emerging automotive cycle. The author quoted a number of security analysts, economic forecasters and university based researchers. All expressed a degree of frustration and certainly a diversity of opinions about whether sales would be up, down or sideways in North America. The root of the analyst's problem is derived from the fact that the industry is going through a significant "structural" change.

In the past, the industry has always experienced "cyclical" change. The auto sector has always been cyclical and will always be cyclical. Therefore, almost everyone who belongs to the Society of Auto Analysts has been immersed in studying these cycles, and have become quite competent at predicting them. The underlying variables are very well understood. However, the issue they all face today, is the emergence of structural change in the industry. Structural change is very difficult to "model" and to forecast. And this is why everyone is so uneasy with their current forecasts.

The key structural change variable can be summed up in one word ... "QUALITY." The Japanese introduced high quality vehicles into North America in the 1980's. By the end of the 1980's virtually everyone had significantly increased their quality levels. The present particular auto cycle is unique, in that consumers for the first time are driving high quality vehicles. This is quite a structural change. During each previous downturn, consumers would delay their auto purchase for various economic reasons by one, two or three years, but at the end of the down cycle, they had no choice but to go out and buy a new or newer vehicle due to the poor quality of their existing vehicle. From a market perspective, quality has given the consumer a "choice" for the first time. Consumers now have an option they never had before. They do not have to buy a new or newer vehicle, they can delay and delay and delay. In Canada, many have delayed their next vehicle purchase by seven years. In the US, they have returned to the market very slowly.

During each and every previous auto cycle, the consumer exploded back into the marketplace. The lowest first year growth after the trough year was 18 percent and in some years it was as high as 25 percent. The lowest second year growth was 10 percent and in some years it was as high as 15 percent. Only in year 3 and 4 did growth start to sputter out a bit. During the most recent auto cycle, the market in North America was up 4 percent the first year, 6.3 percent in the second year and eight percent the third year, while dropping back by about 4 percent in 1995. This recovery is absolutely unique. Because of the structural change, caused by quality, we have seen 18-20 percent of total growth after the trough year, compared to the 40-50 percent growth in every previous cycle. One can understand why the auto analysts are so confused and uncertain about their forecasts.

Because of "quality," the consumer has equity in their vehicle that they never had before. They can use the equity in their vehicles in two different ways. The consumers we talk to fall into one of two groups. The economic disadvantaged consumer (those who are out of a job, or have experienced a wage decrease or job insecurity) takes the equity in their vehicle and they maintain their standard of living. If you buy a used vehicle, the average cost is $10,000 or a carrying cost of some $2,000 to $3,000 per year. If you buy a new vehicle, the average cost is $20,000 or a carrying cost of some $5,000 to $6,000 per year. By not buying a new or used vehicle, the consumer benefits anywhere from $2,000 to $6,000 in after tax purchasing power to maintain their standard of living.

The other consumer group consists of those that are still relatively economically secure. They take the equity in their vehicle and they spend it on other things. Kitchen renovations are currently at the top of the list. But, things like retirement investments, starting/buying a business also rank very high. Consumers are able to buy these items because they don't have to buy a car.

As I look at the market I have come to believe that the critical variable to monitor relative to vehicle sales is vehicle scrappage. Scrappage is obviously very sensitive to the "quality" issue. It also is sensitive to insurance industry write-off policies, accident rates, repair costs and so on. I used to believe that auto sales began with a new vehicle purchase and flowed through two or three used vehicle sales, and finally to a vehicle being scrapped. However, I have come to believe that the entire auto sales cycle begins with a vehicle being scrapped (high scrappage years occur when a vehicle reaches its 10th year). This creates a compelling need to go out and buy a vehicle. But this consumer doesn't usually buy new. Instead, this vehicle owner goes out and buys a newer vehicle, say eight to ten years old. The previous owner of the eight to ten year old vehicle buys a five to seven year old car, the previous owner buys a two to three year old and finally this consumer buys new. In essence, we have a replacement demand market that begins with a vehicle being scrapped. In North America, somewhere between 85 and 90 percent of new vehicle sales are the direct result of a vehicle being scrapped.

In North America today (excluding Mexico since we cannot get any data), there are close to 80 million vehicles on the road which are at least 10 years old. This has never been higher. Again, this large volume of older vehicles is the direct result of higher quality levels.

These older vehicles are now beginning to come off the road in record numbers. The owners of these scrapped vehicles are the owners who buy used and not new, therefore, there is a lot of activity in the used vehicle market. Ultimately, the ripple effect caused by vehicle scrappage should work through the sales cycle and eventually result in the purchase of a new vehicle.

There is a lot of debate over scrappage rates, but scrappage should be between 14 and 16 million units per year for the next five or six years. This will create a floor level below which sales will have a hard time falling. Especially since there is no evidence of fewer vehicles per household, drivers licenses issued continue to grow and kilometres driven have not fallen. To be sure, none of these variables are growing at the rate they achieved in previous decades, but none of them are falling.

There is also some growth in vehicle sales related to demographic and economic growth. This represents about one million units per year. There is also six to eight million units of pent-up demand in the North American market. Pent-up demand is being captured at the rate of 1.5 to 2.0 million units per year.

Therefore, I do not see a sharp drop in the market. I see the three different elements of demand supporting a reasonably healthy market. Replacement demand of 14 to 16 million units per year, pent-up demand of 1.5 to 2.0 million units per year and demographic demand of upwards to 1.5 million units per year.

I see a soft market, but a market that will continue to grow through to the end of the decade. The strength of the scrappage variable limits the downside risk. The market could be off by a million units, but if this happens it will only be a delay in the market and these units will flow through in the following years.

Consumer Auto Purchases Last Recession (1982/83) vs. *Consumer Auto Purchases Recently (1994/95)*	
1982/83	*1994/95*
"No Choice"	"Choice"
Poor Quality Vehicles	High Quality
Low Technology	Great Technology
Rust	Better Integrity
And...	*But...*
Low Debt	High Debt

Average Growth in North America		
	Previous Cycles	This Cycle
1st year	18 to 25%	4.0%
2nd year	10 to 15%	6.3%
3rd year	5 to 10%	8.0%
4th year	2 to 5%	-2.0%

NORTH AMERICAN VEHICLE MARKET OUTLOOK

Pent-up demand conditions will ensure continuing profits

By Dennis Desrosiers

In January, the *Wall Street Journal* and the Canadian *Financial Post* both published articles that reported that the upside for vehicle sales in North America was over. These articles used the standard fears over increasing interest rates, some plant closings, rising inventories and of course interviews with car dealers who were complaining about a lack of profits and slow showroom traffic. However, nowhere did they mention that the auto sector had one of its best years on record in 1994. Everywhere I look I see records, records and near records, be they in the market, production, vehicle companies or parts companies. The US market grew by 8.4 percent; its fourth best year on record and 1.5 million units below its peak potential. The Canadian market, which is two years behind the US recovery, grew by 5.8 percent and is still at least 300,000 units below its peak potential. The Mexico market was up by 7.5 percent and reached 615,000 units, an all time record. The benefits from this stellar performance were shared almost equally across the "Big 3" vehicle companies with:

• GM up by 7.6 percent
• Ford up by 7.4 percent; and
• Chrysler up by 7.8 percent

The import nameplates outperformed the "Big 3" with sales up 9.9 percent, and a substantial portion of their sales were sourced in North America as the New North American Production levels reached a new record of 2.4 million units (this figure excludes Mexico).

Before we call this recovery over, I think it is worthwhile examining previous recoveries. I have tracked each since 1960 and this recovery is the weakest by far in the last 30 years. There have been six auto cycles in that time period, and in each of the previous five we have experienced double digit growth during the first year of recovery. In this cycle the market grew by only four percent. The second year and third year also underperformed the average. The stakeholders, the vehicle companies and their dealers, the Federal Reserve and Bank of Canada and the fiscal policy decision makers, are all managing this recovery better than any previous economic recovery?

In fact, I can build a very strong case that higher interest rates in 1994 were good for the auto sector, not bad. The vehicle companies could not have handled double digit growth and a slowing down of the market may allow the industry to have sustainable growth through to 1997 and possibly 1998, rather than exceptionally high sales in 1994. There are still a number of very healthy signs which indicate three or four years of growth may be possible:

• Currently 75 million vehicles are on the road in Canada and the US which are over 10 years old.

• Mexico (a rough guess) would add 6 million to this total which have to be replaced over the next five to eight years. This will establish a base level of demand of 13 to 16 million units per year.

•Because of the very low growth rates in this recovery, the market has just

North American Market Last 6 Cycles
(includes Mexico)

Trough Year	Growth Rate During First 3 Years After Trough		
	Ist Year	2nd Year	3rd Year
1961	18.80%	9.90%	14.80%
1967	15.20	0.70	20.30
1971	20.30	9.60	8.80
1975	18.90	10.90	4.20
1983	14.50	19.10	10.70
1991	4.00	6.30	8.30

Source: DesRosiers Automotive Consultants & Wards

reached trend line demand (4th quarter 1994) in North America. This means that the pent-up demand created by the last recession (approximately 7.5 million units) has just begun to be drawn upon. The recapturing of this pent-up demand adds further credence to continued growth in the market. However, it would be foolish to ignore the downside risks in today's market:

• Higher interest rates which increase the cost of borrowing for a new car and reduce or delay sales.

• Exchange rates, which have more of an impact in Canada and Mexico than in the US market, will negatively impact sales in 1995.

North American Sales of Vehicles-Number of Units
(Includes Heavy Duty Truck)

Year	US	Canada	Mexico	North America	Canada as a % of North America	Mexico as a % of North America
1990	14148404	1314118	544930	16005452	8.2	3.4
1991	12541321	1287056	642981	14471358	8.9	4.4
1992	13117848	1227841	706914	15052601	8.2	4.7
1993	14202858	1188992	603067	15994917	7.4	3.8
1994	15415239	1250373	615130	17280742	7.2	3.6
1995 Forecast	15800000	1320000	500000	17620000	7.5	2.8
1996 Forecast	16200000	1425000	550000	18175000	7.8	3.0
1997 Forecast	16500000	1498000	625000	18623000	8.0	3.4
1998 Forecast	15800000	1517195	700000	18017195	8.4	3.9
1999 Forecast	15500000	1449000	725000	17674000	8.2	4.1

• Governments, which continue to target the vehicle for increased taxes and regulatory costs, will further decrease affordability.

• General uncertainty, which exists especially in Canada and Mexico, undermines consumer confidence and may further delay new vehicle purchases.

All of these factors are negative and will take some growth out of the market but should not result in a decline. We therefore are forecasting about a two percent growth in North America with Canada, the strongest market, and Mexico the weakest. I estimate downside risk in this forecast of up to one million units. Since this drop, if it happens, would come after a very good year, the market would still be relatively strong at about 16.5 million units. I believe the probability of this is low but if it happens, then the lost sales, including those lost to the current interest rate bubble, will be pushed out into 1996, 1997 and 1998. We could see short term pain for long term gain.

PUSHING THE LIMITS OF DESIGN

Every January, The Detroit International Auto Show has been the showcase for advances in automotive technology. Not only have electrical vehicles, as well as gas/electrical hybrids been launched in great admiration in the 1990s, but the aesthetic and aerodynamic quality of the vehicles themselves has substantially improved. Legendary auto designer, Sergio Pininfarina, came to the Detroit Auto Show in 1999, with the view that design elements will come to play more important roles over the next decade when quality levels between brands converge even further.

In "Ferrari at 50," one of the best managed brand names in the world, is presented as having a sound underlying business strategy through the appointment of a number of key people "with a passion for the brand" in decision-making positions. The fusion of style, brand name and glorious racing history is an unbeatable combination that is the envy of even the "Big 3." Ferrari will be the role model in which many existing brands will try to emulate to ensure success.

In "Canadian SuperCar," a start up company was profiled as a potential competitor to the Ferrari's of the world. Although very impressive in design and aesthetics, the car carried a very complex brand name in "MCV-CH4." Ultimately, success required more than just design and beauty to establish an upscale market presence. The history of Ferrari and the advertising budget of General Motors for one, would have greatly benefited the cause.

W.b.z.V.

AUTOMOTIVE DESIGN TRENDS
Classic Cars Embrace High Technology in Detroit

William B.Z. Vukson

Detroit has become the world's pre-eminent automotive show. Held very early in the new year, it sets a standard that is very rarely matched by the series of auto shows held throughout the year around the world in places like Geneva, Tokyo, London and Frankfurt. The importance of the Detroit show has become universally accepted by even European auto manufacturers, which is reflected by their choice of Detroit's venue for unveiling some of the most important new models and concept cars that will come to define contemporary design and technology trends. Of this select group of European manufacturers, it is only the large German producers; Volkswagen-Audi, Mercedes-Benz and BMW, that have invested heavily in a North American presence, arguing that in today's global environment they can only succeed by developing a solid US sales performance. This philosophy is not shared, however, by French producers Peugeot-Citroën and Renault and by Italian industrial powerhouse, Fiat, which also produces the Lancia and attractive Alfa-Romeo brand names within its group. In that respect, the European based auto shows in Paris, Frankfurt and Geneva are unique to the extent that design and production trends in the French and Italian auto industries are not directly witnessed by North American viewers and buyers.

The recent merger of Daimler Benz with Chrysler Corporation will ensure that the German presence in North America accelerates even further. Not only will Mercedes-Benz cars become identified more and more with the American buying public, the continued shifting of production by BMW to the US market will continue to follow its very impressive sales trend. Joining its German counterparts will be Volkswagen-Audi, as the success of the new Beetle is bound to be joined by the growing appeal of the Audi name brand once again. The North American introduction of the Audi TT coupe is a case in point, with its original introduction as a concept car in 1995, it is slated to become a very attractive production car in the year 2000 with a 180 horsepower, 1.8 litre turbocharged five-valve engine coupled with a five-speed manual transmission. Joining the Audi TT Coupe, the Detroit show witnessed the worldwide introductions of a restyled Buick LeSabre; a new BMW X5 sport activity vehicle produced at its production plant in Spartanburg, South Carolina, and the launch of the new Chevrolet Impala. North American vehicle introductions included the European Ford Focus; Jaguar S-Type; Mercedes-Benz S-Class; Nissan Xterra; Saab 9-5 Wagon and the re-designed Volkswagen Cabrio, Golf and Jetta. Later in 1999, Volkswagen will offer the Jetta with a turbo-diesel engine that attains up to 49 miles to one US gallon.

Design Trends Through Concept Vehicles

Two noticeable trends in design were evident at the Detroit show. The unveiling of the Chrysler "PT Cruiser" concept vehicle was consistent to this year's theme of "category busters" or vehicles that defy being categorised as either a car, truck, sport utility or minivan, but rather straddle two or more of these segments. Ford's newly redesigned "Thunderbird" reflects a reversion back to the automobiles of the 1950s. The new Thunderbird concept vehicle is a modern interpretation of a classic American icon, something that the designers at Ford call "modern-heritage." According to Ford; "There are only a select few nameplates that have earned their way into the hearts of the motoring public by establishing a true heritage. Thunderbird is certainly one of them." The project direction was to recreate the enthusiasm of the original by building a two-seat roadster with Thunderbird elements, but in a distinctly modern interpretation. In the words of Ford; "Today's Thunderbird concept salutes the original but also symbolizes turn-of-the-millennium automotive styling."

The Cadillac division of General Motors has unveiled a concept car that it hopes will define the design trend for its flagship division. The Cadillac Evoq is a luxury V8-powered roadster that is the first true Cadillac concept car in more than a decade. The "Evoq" is intended to capture the emotion of great Cadillacs of the past, but in a totally forward-looking way. The Evoq is designed as a rear-wheel-drive two-seater with a retractable hardtop, blending in with its "crisply tailored lines that establish an expressive design direction for future Cadillac models."

Technology to Redefine the Marketplace

1999 is the year when all of the technological advances introduced to the public at the Detroit show hits the marketplace. From the first battery-powered electrical concept vehicles early in the decade to the later refinements that merged electricity with the gasoline-powered engine, forming a "hybrid," most of the major auto producers are ready to offer the consumers their version of a technologically-advanced mass production vehicle. The "Honda Hybrid" is one of the first of these vehicles that is able to boast 70 miles to one US gallon of gasoline in both city and highway driving. The Honda VV hybrid incorporates a three cylinder engine with an Integrated Motor Assist (IMA) system along with weight reducing materials and technologies. Honda claims that this will be one of the most technically sophisticated mass production vehicles ever made. A complex electronics package handles the automated charging, engine assist and electric current generation, which promises to be completely transparent to the vehicle's occupants.

In the concept vehicle category, the Cadillac Evoq features a new tire mounting technology from Michelin called the "Pax System" which relies on clamping forces around the rim that promises to reduce rolling resistance and improve fuel economy. In addition, it enhances safety since the tire is anchored to the rim even in a "flat" hazard situation. The Evoq also features a "Night Vision" feature. This thermal-imaging technology helps the driver detect potentially dangerous situations well beyond the range of the vehicle's headlamps. Cadillac claims to be the first to introduce the safety benefits of this technology to drivers by offering the Night Vision feature on the year 2000 DeVille model range.

AUTO DESIGN TRENDS
Pininfarina, Bertone & ItalDesign go to Detroit

William B.Z. Vukson

In one of the most powerful displays of technological achievement and wondrous design, the Detroit International Auto Show assembled a trio of legendary Italian car designers. In the words of Sergio Pininfarina: "the Detroit show has begun to attract an international audience," and that "auto design will begin to command a far more prominent role" in the manufacturing and marketing process across all brands.

Pininfarina was joined by colleagues Paolo Caccamo of Bertone and Giorgetto Giugiaro of ItalDesign. Bertone is known for the design and production of the famous Alfa Romeo Giulietta Coupe, the Fiat X1/9 Spyder (best selling Italian sports car in North America) and the Lamborghini Miura and the Countach among some of the high performance cars. In the field of styling, Bertone has worked for Alfa Romeo, Fiat, Mazda, Daewoo, Volvo and the French manufacturer, Citroën. Likewise, ItalDesign is known for the design of such makes as the De Lorean, Fiat Panda, UNO and Punto, the first Volkswagen Golf, the Lexus GS300 and the inspiring Lotus Esprit.

In the case of Pininfarina, the most notable production cars have been the Fiat and Alpha Spyder, numerous Ferrari models, including the Daytona and Testarossa and now the Peugeot 306 convertible; the Peugeot 406 Coupe and the Bentley Azure. Pininfarina has been designing production models for Fiat, Lancia, Alfa Romeo, Ferrari, General Motors, Honda, Rolls Royce and Peugeot of France. More than 30 million cars of the Pininfarina design have been built around the world.

Displayed at the Detroit show were recent prototypes of each company. Bertone's Kayak with Lancia K mechanical components was joined by the Karisma with Porsche 911 mechanical components, while ItalDesign brought the Bugatti EB 112 and the Shighera; which enlivens the myth of the legendary Alfa Romeo sports cars. Pininfarina, according to his words, exhibited two samples of "aesthetic research:" the Argento Vivo, which combined a sporty car with the rationality of a sophisticated make like Honda and the Peugeot "Nautilus." The Nautilus was designed and built to show that a classical theme like that of a four door saloon vehicle of high performance can also carry a new and very distinctive personality and a strong sport image.

Not only is the automobile industry making great strides in technological advancement in engine performance and fuel economy, not to mention the recent commercialisation of electrical vehicles, but the design element in the words of Pininfarina "will become more and more important, perhaps the most aggressive factor in sales promotion."

FERRARI AT 50

Interview with: **Gian Luigi Longinotti Buitoni,**
President & CEO
Ferrari North America Inc.

Directed by: **William B.Z. Vukson**

Despite recession Ferrari has introduced two new models- the F355 & F512 M in this their 50th anniversary year. The appointment in 1992 of Gian Luigi Longinotti Buitoni as the President & CEO of North American operations, has shifted the overall strategy back to the customer with an aggressive emphasis on servicing Ferrari's existing clientele.

Who are Ferrari's clients?

They come from a wide variety of backgrounds, but are normally aged from 40 to 45 years, 80 percent of whom are self-employed entrepreneurs with an annual income in excess of $500,000 and a net worth of $3.0 million. Furthermore, about 70 percent tend to be repeat customers.

Is this not a little on the high side?

Three years ago we were selling cars to the wrong customers, as speculators during the "bubble" years were naturally drawn to our cars as more of a social statement. They weren't enjoying the car, however, now we are back to our real buyers.

Is there a large proportion of leased vehicles on the market?

No. We see about 95 percent in cash transactions and only five percent are financed in various ways.

Where is the Ferrari automobile manufactured and what is the yearly production volume?

They are all produced in Italy and consist of a yearly turnover of 3000 to 4000 vehicles on average.

What is a general geographical breakdown in your overall sales patterns?

North America is the most important market for us, which accounts for about 25 percent of overall sales. This is followed in importance by Germany which takes 20 percent of the sales figure, Italy composes 17 percent and Switzerland about 10 percent, followed by Japan and France.

How important are the emerging markets for Ferrari?

We see a lot of the sales in central and eastern European countries registered through the German sales reports. In addition, we have opened new offices in Moscow and Beijing recently. Up to now, four cars have been sold from our Moscow dealership and have recently completed our first sale in Beijing.

Are there any markets that have been disappointing recently?

Yes, the Italian sales figures have been hit very hard due to on-going financial and political crises. For instance, sales in 1992 have been at 1000 vehicles, which we all know is far too much on the high side, compared to about 400 in 1993.

I must stress here that it is vital that one looks at the average three year figure in order to obtain the true performance trend over the longer term. In the Italian case, 600 vehicles sold per annum is a more reasonable number that we have come to expect.

Has the lira weakness increased exports from your production site in Italy?

It helps somewhat, but the price is usually fixed in dollars in the North American market at the dealer level, so that if the lira declines any further, the exchange difference is kept by the Maranello factory in Italy.

Also, since a good part of our clientele is established repeat customers, any differences that may be passed on due to exchange rate fluctuations would only have marginal effects.

There seems to be a small revolution at the dealer level, ever since you have stressed the importance in having your dealers fully participate from a technical side in the Challenge racing series. Why do you have this attitude toward the dealer network?

We believe that Ferrari dealers should participate in racing to support the Ferrari image, to get to know our customers better and to gain service know-how under such circumstances. I am prepared to weed out all dealers that are not devoted enough, since 80 percent of our business is generated with only 30 percent of our dealers.

Service is more important than ever for Ferrari, both as a profit center and in terms of customer satisfaction and retention now that new sales volumes are lower than in past years.

CANADIAN SUPERCAR
MCV-CH4 High Performance/High Tech Vehicle

Interview with: **Robert J. Waddell,**
                      President
                      Motion Concept Vehicles Inc.
Directed by: **William B.Z. Vukson**

The first Canadian based luxury road vehicle plans to enter the production stage in the summer of 1995 and be in competition with some of the world's finest luxury name brand vehicles

How did Motion Concept Vehicles (MCV) begin?

A group of automotive enthusiastic investors had a vision of building a world-class Canadian-based sports car. Canadian sports cars in the past have never been properly manufactured and marketed as high-end road vehicles.

In addition, our goal was to mix composite aerospace technology together with the use of a clean fuel such as natural gas. In this respect, Canadians have never really been recognized in the racing world, yet some of the best automotive technology is based in southern Ontario.

Why would this new automobile succeed against some of the more established names in this market, such as Ferrari or Lamborghini?

I believe that it will succeed because of its unique combination of technologies. The use of composite materials, and it being a clean-running car, not to mention its attractive styling features. In addition, its price will be less than what competitors are charging.

What does its title MCV-CH4 represent?

MCV stands for Motion Concept Vehicles which describes what we are intending to do with the company, which is to build our own car and to get involved in the engineering and development of other prototypes. This latter point is where the Concept comes in.

Motion applies to our interest in the broader participation in road-going transport vehicles, and the CH4 represents the chemical composition of methane-the technological side of the vehicles name.

What is the nature of the market for this type of vehicle?

Its a small niche market and worldwide would have a sell-through capacity of some 2000 vehicles per annum.

We hope to capture some four percent of this market internationally, or sell about 80 vehicles per annum over the longer term. The Canadian portion will represent about ten vehicles of this overall total. In addition, we will be looking towards the Asian market to generate a good deal of interest.

What would be the vehicles' retail price?

We expect it to be between $250,000 and $300,000 Canadian dollars per vehicle, depending on the level of the exchange rate with the US dollar. Since some parts, such as the composite material used in the chassis is imported from the US.

What is the significance of the design chosen?

First of all, it is designed by Jay Bernard, who is based in Canada. In terms of the styling, it is a classical cab-forward variety, made famous by some recent models produced on a massive scale by Chrysler. Moreover, with the engine located behind the driver, it pushes the driver forward, but it also gives good weight distribution from front to rear, with the engine above the driving wheels for better traction. These were the initial parameters that later inspired the actual design.

Was the design inspired by any existing vehicle on the market, or was it designed completely from scratch?

It was designed entirely from scratch. There may be elements from a number of different vehicles already existing. The unique feature is the design of the sides.

How long has the development process lasted to this point?

We first began the project in 1989, but have been involved on a full-time basis for the last three years.

Has there been any previous attempts at bringing such a vehicle to market in Canada?

Not to my knowledge. However, there have been very successful race-car projects in the past, but I am not aware of any road cars.

How has the project been funded to date?

It has been funded through our company, which takes on various consulting projects to design and develop various automotive products. This has enabled us to fund the project to now by diverting this daily operating cash-flow.

Also, in 1994, a major investor has allowed us to proceed towards the full-running stage of development. However, we are now at a critical point, where we need to fund the production level. This is where a working prototype of the vehicle progresses towards an actual usable and marketable product.

How much capital would be required to go from the running to production stages?

We estimate that it would take approximately ten million Canadian dollars, for the initial inventory of vehicles to be produced.

Do you have any committed orders at this point in time?

We have a number of interested inquiries at this preliminary running stage. However, it is very important to have it fully functioning so that prospective clients can feel and hear the vehicle. At that point, we can begin to canvass solid purchase commitments.

Based on our market research we are currently planning 15 to 20 cars per annum initially, increasing to 80 vehicles after a four year period.

How would the vehicle be distributed throughout the world?

Initially, through a very few selective exotic car dealers in North America, Europe and Asia. We also plan to present the car at the upcoming Geneva automotive show, in order to raise the distributor's level of interest in it.

PHOTO GALLERY

Top left: French President Jacques Chirac with late Italian Prime-Minister Bettino Craxi

Top right: Former German Chancellor Helmut Kohl with French President Jacques Chirac

Above: UN operations in the Balkans

Bottom left: Anti-Corruption Magistrate Antonio DiPietro (centre)

Bottom right: Seven times former Prime-Minister of Italy Giulio Andreotti on trial for Mafia association

Top left, opposite page: Gerald Lacoste, CEO of the Montreal Exchange

Top right, opposite page:Sir Samuel Brittan, assistant editor, Financial Times of London

Bottom left, opposite page: Tihomir Mikulic, managing director, Kapital Trade

Bottom right, opposite page: Giovanni Giarrusso, advisor to emerging stock markets

Top left: Chris Cviic, former editor, The Economist

Top right: Dr. Michele Fratianni, Professor and staff advisor to Ronald Reagan

Right: Peter Galbraith, former U.S. Ambassador to Croatia with Yasushi Akashi, special U.N. envoy to Bosnia

A

Abdullah, Crown Prince, *70*
Achille Lauro, *3*
AC Milan, *97*
AGIP, *72*
Alfa-Romeo, *147*
Aloha Airlines, *54*
Anatolian, *64*
Andreotti, Giulio *1, 2-4, 6*
APEC (Asia Pacific Economic Cooperation), *14, 49*
Aran Energy, *72*
Arizona, *9*
Asian Tigers, *13*
AT&T, *68*
Australia, *67, 114, 121, 124*
Austria, *27, 79*
Aziz, King Fahd Bin Abdul , *68*
Aziz, Tariq, *72*

B

Balance of Trade, *8, 60*
Balladur, Edouard, *2, 7, 8*
Bank for International Settlements (BIS), *119*
Bank of Canada, *138, 144*
Bank of England, *38, 39, 113, 114, 117, 118, 122, 123, 131, 132*
Bank of France, *16, 25, 26, 44*
Bank of Japan, *10*
Banque Nationale de Paris, *453*
Barings, *38, 105, 114, 116, 121, 123, 124, 130-134*
Baring Brothers & Co., Limited, *133*
Barings Crisis, *38*
Barings Securities Limited, *133*
Berlin, *1, 84*
Berlusconi, Silvio, *1, 6, 97, 99, 96*
Bertone, *149, 150*
Bible Belt, *95*
Bildt, Carl, *75, 76*
BMW, *147*
Bokassa, Emperor, *7*
Boeing, *9, 68*

Bosnia, *73-80, 109*
Bossi, Umberto, *99*
Bretton Woods, *29, 87, 90*
British Airways, *54*
Brittan, Sir Samuel, *17, 36*
Brazil, *13, 72*
Bundesbank, German, *20, 25, 44*
Burma, *82*
Bush, George, *1, 49, 85, 91*
Business Travellers, *54*

C

Caccamo, Paolo, *149*
Cadillac Evoq, *148*
California, *3, 9*
Calvi, Roberto, *2*
Canada Deposit Insurance Corporation (CDIC), *117, 118, 120*
Canale Cinque, *97*
CAP (Common Agricultural Policy), *18, 24*
Capital Mobility, *21, 66*
Carter Administration, *52*
Caselli, Giancarlo, *4*
Central Banks, Independent, *32*
Chapter, *57, 47*
Chiesa, Carlo Alberto Dalla, *2*
China, *9, 13, 70, 82*
Christian Democratic Party, *2, 5, 6*
Chaban-Delmas, Jacques, *7*
Chirac, Jacques, *8, 72*
Chretien, Prime Minister Jean, *59*
Christie's, *106*
City of London, *41*
Civil Law, *92*
Civil War, *80, 94, 95*
Clinton, Bill, *9, 49, 90-96*
Clinton, Hillary, *91*
CN Rail, *58*
Cold War, *1, 12, 48, 82, 93, 16, 81, 96*
(CDLR) Committee for the Defense of Legitimate Rights, *69*
Countervailing Duties, *65*
Craxi, Bettino, *1, 6*
Currency Risk, *46*